PHILOSOPHICAL ESSAYS

Michael D. Halliday

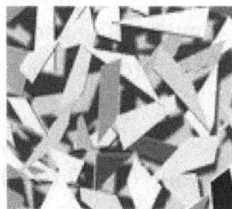

SHARDS PUBLISHING

First Published 2014 by Shards Publishing.

Copyright © 2014 Michael D. Halliday

British Library Cataloguing in Publication Data.
A catalogue record of this book is available from the British Library.

IBSN. 978-0-9568124-4-5

Authors OnLine Ltd.
19 The Cinques,
Gamlingay,Sandy,
Bedfordshire, SG 19 3NU,
England.

(Telephone 01767 652005).

The book is also available in e-book format, details from www.authorsonline.co.uk

Dedication

For my darling daughters
Justine and Lorna

ACKNOWLEDGEMENTS

As always, my profound gratitude, love, and admiration go to my partner, Joyce Margaret Davies, who kindly typed the Manuscript and mopped my fevered brow.

CONTENTS

PHILOSOPHICAL ESSAYS

INTRODUCTION

The general aim was to write a book which makes sense of the main features of philosophy, on the hopefully non-contentious assumption that it is possible to do so. This must be open to doubt, because one of the things that can get philosophy a bad name is that professional philosophers can hardly agree about anything at all, even on the nature of their own subject. At any rate the author has attempted to give a clear idea of what he believes plausible philosophy to be, and also how to do it in practice.

Since the author was trained as a physical scientist who has dabbled in philosophy, the book will probably be of more interest to practising scientists than professional philosophers. The main audience, however, is likely to be that indispensable friend of the non-fiction writer - the 'intelligent layman'.

So why yet another book on philosophy when there are so many out there already? Partly there is vanity, of course, but mostly it is out of frustration with the predictable and unoriginal, as well as quite frankly, difficult and uncommunicative, tomes on offer from the all- too- erudite professional practitioners in the field. In short, the goal was to write the kind of book the author would himself have liked to learn from had it been available.

INTRODUCTION

In fairness, however, to quote the Oxford philosopher P. F. Strawson: 'There is no such thing as elementary philosophy. There is no shallow end to the philosophical pool.' (Analysis and Metaphysics).

Every subject in the present Essays is considered in a focused and condensed way, confining it to essential detail only, and avoiding exploratory discussion of the legion, subordinate issues which could be explored almost without limit. It is hoped that, once readers understand the perspective on philosophy that the book seeks to provide, they will wish to investigate further some of the fruitful 'byways' for themselves, whilst desirably avoiding the numerous pitfalls of method, as well as the more unhinged and fanciful ideas, which the book should help readers to spot more easily.

The author wishes that all thinking adults would take the time consciously to develop their own philosophical and scientific worldview, in order to become genuinely autonomous as people in the world. But they would be fooling themselves if they uncritically accepted ideas in the process which were relatively unsupported, tempting as a lack of rigour may sometimes be. We all have lazy minds at least part of the time and the author can be no exception, unfortunately. So vigilance should be our perennial watchword.

1. QUEST

The World-Riddle

'Sooner or later', writes Maurice Riesling, 'life makes philosophers of us all.'
'There is not one of us who is not trying to make sense of his existence, and at some level of our being each is seeking fulfilment. Our experiences come pouring into us with endless variety, and they do not come neatly packaged and labelled. Each one of us must select and assimilate, organise and arrange, value and apply. So if we have awakened, we are all philosophers by default, not by choice. To be sure we may seek the guidance of others who have searched. But in the last analysis, we must find our own answers and meanings.'

James L. Christian - Philosophy:
The Art of Wondering

A main intention of the book is to encourage readers to go on a philosophical Quest. The term 'quest' of the chapter title is an interesting one. It denotes a search, often in the grandiose sense of a perhaps major undertaking. Sometimes it takes on the mantle of a mission, like a religious crusade or pilgrimage. It may stand for an adventure, frequently a geographical exploration involving travel, maybe to places exotic or unknown. It is massively important and portentous, so we address it with a capital Q.

Literature - from ancient mythological tales to contemporary stories - is the archetypal source of 'the Quest' in popular understanding. There is much made of the idea in Tolkien's 'The Lord of the Rings', for example, as well as in the well-known Arthurian legends, some of which centre on the Quest for the Holy Grail.

But the Quest in literature may serve just as a simple excuse around which to build a plot and justify a journey, having no especially worthwhile purpose. This reminds of a liberal view in Education that what is of value is 'process' rather than any end achievement. The author clearly repudiates the idea in his own espousal of questing, whilst acknowledging the instrumental importance of process in each context notwithstanding.

The driven individual is easy to caricature, of course, few more effectively than Don Quixote, the errant subject of Miguel de Cervantes' great Spanish novel and a man sufficiently deluded as to tilt with his broken lance at windmills. There is much to learn here, especially of a cautionary nature, for the tales are rich in the drama of futility, a comically sad study of the failures that stem from a lack of object, or too undiscriminating a focus. The Quest can also be over large, as when Quixote says he plans to destroy injustice itself! The Quest as literary device is here used partly as a vehicle to mock Quixote, a hero and lovable 'knight' no doubt, but a fool nevertheless.

QUEST

It should not be drawn from this that Quests are only for idiots, or inevitably result in complete distortion of a life, though the latter is certainly a risk for such people as the excessively selfish, eccentrics, and the obsessive. Quixote's path, we are amused to see, is all too likely to lead to a less than firm grasp on Reality. And that way madness lies ... .

Yet its heroism, together with a very human weakness not to live up to the concept in practice at times, are also lessons we can take from the novel for the pursuance of our (philosophical) lives. As is a kind of dedication born in the single-minded.

It may not always be easy for others to acquiesce in contemplation of such a personality; his Quest may seem quite singular and therefore odd, pathological even. There will be those who claim it signifies a wasted life, notwithstanding that the individual concerned may find a deep fulfilment by it.

Not all literature is fantasy, of course, and not all underplays the importance of Quest for an ordinary life. Rather, the ideas being encouraged here point up the positive aspects of the Quest such as stem from wisdom gained and character developed. Note that the central figure in Salinger's modern American novel 'The Catcher in the Rye', Holden Caulfield, undertakes a common enough rite of passage into adulthood where, hopefully, he will find a sense of purpose and learn to reason in a more balanced way. There is frequently some lack in a person's life which motivates a desire for satisfaction through a Quest.

Henry David Thoreau, a nineteenth century American writer with a philosophical turn of mind, advised 'pursue, keep up with, circle round and round your life, as a dog does his master.' This suggests active, but somewhat fixated purpose, one that does not swerve from its aim, to which it is entirely loyal. It is consistent with a Quest that is about oneself as a whole, whereas a more practicable approach could be to devise parallel or serial 'projects', splitting up the so-called 'balanced life' into categories of involvement, such as those of work, family, friends, health and fitness, travel, and hobbies. These projects can be of long or short duration, with varying degrees of sophistication and time involvement, of course.

Such an approach is anathema to many, who baulk at a planned life with a lot of structure and routine. Some artistic temperaments, swayed by large swings of mood, might have a Quest alright, but accompanied by a tendency to waste time by meandering and emotional indulgence. In principle it is a good deal easier for the organised and linear thinkers, those scientifically trained to be methodical, logical, and systematic.

Psychologists will no doubt point to the therapeutic benefits, as well as dangers, of a life dominated by a Quest, or maybe a series of them no less. Some people, such as the present author, have a naturally questing outlook, while others are not so consciously purposive, more inclined to drift, not obviously ambitious or directive in relation to goals, aims, or targets.

A clear advantage of the Quest is that, whilst it can skew or redirect the emphases in a life certainly, it also provides a basis for the allocation and justification of an individual's precious time between what can be many pressing and competing demands. Yet it is important to understand that the Quest as here discussed is not really a mundane matter; rather it lifts the mind above the humdrum. One of its tricks for a successful outcome will be to anchor it in some kind of firm bedrock. Insights and activities need to be properly grounded, not floating free in an imaginary realm of far-fetched hopes and dreams, where enchantment and bewitchment can deceive.

Now it is both here, as well as commonly, implied that a Quest has noble character and some difficulty, hence uncertainty, of achievement. That is all to the good in the present context, because the philosophical outlook and life are not easy. They strive for wisdom and truth, so how could matters be otherwise?

It may be a mistake, finally, to look within the Quest itself for personal happiness. Popularly seen as a much more obvious and natural goal, happiness is usually viewed by philosophers as at best elusive. And, because life is a struggle, and because of the grim limitations of the human condition, it is all too transient if, or when, it comes. No, the grand Quest has quite a different end in view; it seeks for greatness, inevitably fails, but possibly for all that raises us up just a little of the way.

2. WISDOM

Introduction
Wisdom and Happiness
Wisdom and Existence
Defining Wisdom
Wisdom and Philosophy
Wisdom and Ethics
Wisdom and Religion
Wisdom and Literature
Wisdom and the Social Sciences
Becoming Wise
Wisdom and the Future
Wisdom and the Quest

WISDOM

Introduction

We start with an unjustly neglected commodity in the modern world, one in rather short supply, namely wisdom. This should serve to sweep away some preliminary misconceptions and also provide motivating ideals.

It is not the main purpose of the present work to produce an in-depth analysis of wisdom however. Nor does the author presume to know enough about it to become wise himself.

Nevertheless, the chapter does attempt to say just a little about wisdom, partly to point a possible way to it, and mainly to clarify distinctions from, and relations to our philosophical Quest.

Wisdom and Happiness

Herman Hesse, a German-Swiss novelist, claimed that 'Happiness is a how, not a what; a talent, not an object.' The thought is apposite because most people in our society, when asked about their main goal in life, parrot out shallow remarks about the central importance not of wisdom, but happiness. And, of course, nobody is going to advocate that we deliberately pursue a life of misery. So it does seem reasonable, and so far as it goes, it is.

However, as Hesse suggests, happiness is a peculiar business. If it is conceived, as it frequently is, as some sort of positive state of mind which is our normal mode and a lasting disposition, it can prove elusive and temporary.

And there are times when it would be too selfish to be happy. Unless you are remarkably (even pathologically) self-centred, you will not be able to find happiness during a close bereavement, or when the love of your life has rejected you. Neither does happiness necessarily equate with wealth, or with the self-indulgent life of pleasure-seeking either.

Paradoxically, perhaps, shrewd people sometimes say that you find happiness by instead forgetting about it as such whilst pursuing other worthwhile things. So there is an argument for the axiom that wisdom is prior to happiness; that is, of higher value and more fundamental importance.

Wisdom and Existence

Now 'Man is the only animal for whom his own existence is a problem which he has to solve'. So says Erich Fromm, a German psychoanalyst. (We had better add 'on Earth' just to be on the safe side). This is the existentialist problem, of course. Given our variable capacities to make choices, and our differing circumstances in life, just how do we decide on our key paths? Sadly, we often don't. At least we tend to drift, to allow others too big a say, to use the wrong information, or poor reasoning, misleading emotions, and, in short, to proceed without wisdom, a theoretical concept seemingly in very short actual supply in the world.

Defining Wisdom

So what is this thing called wisdom? The thesaurus view is that wisdom broadly has three constituent elements: understanding, knowledge, and prudence (2.1). Implicit here is the notion that a wise person will talk and act appropriately on the basis of sound judgement and relevant knowledge, as well as displaying any desirable caution, circumspection, astuteness, and tact. Francis Hutcheson put it that: 'wisdom denotes the pursuing of the best ends by the best means'. All of these insights about the concept, of course, beg the key valuing questions, such as what may constitute 'best' and 'appropriate' in particular contexts.

Wisdom is said by some to have many facets, associated perhaps with a wide collection of positive human characteristics important for personal and social well-being.

The opposite of wisdom is 'folly', so therein lies a clue. Sometimes wisdom is equated with 'sapience', an 'ability to act with appropriate judgement', probably distinct from intelligence, which does not always lead to it.

The contemporary philosopher, Nicholas Maxwell, defines wisdom as 'the capacity to realize what is of value in life, for oneself and others'. Perhaps that suggests that psychology, sociology, literature, and maybe some other disciplines, are just as likely to be informative about it as philosophy, or even more so, a view strongly endorsed by the author and hopefully evident from the book.

James Christian's philosophical definition is apposite. 'Wisdom is the understanding and skill to make sound judgements about the use of knowledge in the context of daily life - the antidote to foolishness.' And Igor Grossman, a social psychologist, equates wisdom with 'the ability to navigate the important challenges of social life'.

Interesting is the context chosen by the social science 'Defining Wisdom' project of the University of Chicago, which seems to regard wisdom as a sort of superior know-how exhibited by a relatively small proportion of people in social situations, especially perhaps the conflictual ones. This 'wisdom' appears to be related to the kind of wily decision-making used to choose our comments and to govern behaviour designed to be in our own best interests. Some of the key underlying values are characteristics like seeking compromises, admitting uncertainty, being flexible. And these tend to come from those who have the most stable 'emotional intelligence and ability to control feelings' (2.2). The picture bucks popular conceptions of wisdom being equated with truth, or knowing the right answers. Sometimes it amounts to a recognition that there is no right answer, that the situation is in fact intractable.

It also points to the kind of skills that the good psychotherapist will need, such as the ability to listen, to empathise, to reflect dispassionately. It would then follow that considerable prior experience of the vicissitudes of life would be a necessary pre-condition. But that alone would not make a good therapist. There is much formal learning and training to be acquired as well, not least the capacity to ask the right sort of questions and in an acceptable way.

From what has been said, it would seem that wisdom is not confined then in its knowledge component to one given subject. You could be wise (or foolish) in all sorts of situations in life where the prior knowledge requirements would be almost infinitely varied. And it is certainly not part of the 'common understanding' that wisdom is entirely the province of the sciences, logic, or philosophy.

So are there finally any broad conclusions which research can tell us? A survey of four general approaches to the analysis of wisdom as a concept concluded with a tentative theory that:
'S is wise if and only if:
      (1) S has extensive factual and theoretical knowledge,
      (2) S knows how to live well,
      (3) S is successful at living well,
      (4) S has very few unjustified beliefs' (2.3).

But once again an irrepressible subjectivity creeps back in over the seemingly harmless use of deceptively little words like 'well', and the meaning of justified belief.

WISDOM

Wisdom and Philosophy

People very often associate the getting of wisdom with the pursuit of philosophy. And yet it is rare to find the term 'wisdom' mentioned at all in dictionaries of philosophy. And its study is quite parlous in the contemporary discipline. So what is this? It could suggest a temporary falling out of fashion; matters come and go in popularity. Or it might be that wisdom is not an especially suitable concept for philosophical study. The current chapter will attempt to shine a little light.

Now it is true that there is traditionally said to be a connection between philosophy and wisdom. The world 'philosophy' comes from the Greek 'philo' meaning 'love' and 'sophia' meaning 'wisdom'. But 'a love of wisdom' is hardly informative when you don't really know what wisdom is, a classic illustration of the problem of circular definition.

Another idea the general public have is that somehow wisdom is acquired with age, by a vague attribution of what is learned from experience. The notion prompts the suspicion that there is little understanding here of the mechanisms involved. It is true we do know older citizens whose judgement seems well balanced. Equally, there are very many who sadly have little to offer. As with most lessons in life, the likelihood is that some will be very much better at grasping them than others. We shall return to this.

WISDOM

A third popular myth is to believe that just a few people, sometimes referred to as 'sages', are oracles of wisdom for the rest to consult for their insights into life. The sages are usually religious figures. They are rarely even academics, still less professional philosophers. Implicit here is the idea that wise people are in control of their emotions through the power of will. In modern parlance, they exhibit 'emotional intelligence'.

There are modern philosophical writings which do address problems of living. Of these authors, Alain de Botton might be cited in particular, as a philosopher who writes sensitively on the great and perennial problems of the human condition. In 'The Consolations of Philosophy' de Botton helpfully takes some common negative occurrences in life_ such as being unpopular, feeling inadequate, being frustrated, suffering inadequacy, or a broken heart, having financial difficulties - and uses the writings and lives of famous philosophers to provide inspiration for how at least we may mentally come to terms with them. (2.4). It might also be fair to say that philosophical wisdom does not usually leap from the pages of the great philosophers without being dug for like this. And that contemporary professional philosophers seldom address such topics anyway.

In his book 'Conditions of Love' the philosopher, John Armstrong ambitiously explores what is a very complex concept in both theory and practice, as most of us find out to our cost (2.5). This is just the kind of set of issues that philosophy, with its traditions of conceptual analysis, is well placed to help with. Help with, though, not solve in isolation, it has to be admitted.

Wisdom and Ethics

Also a branch of philosophy, ethics has a very significant contribution to make to the getting of wisdom through its Aristotelian tradition of study of the virtues. In his book 'The Great Virtues', the French philosopher, André Comte-Sponville, for instance, outlines the qualities of some eighteen virtues_ like prudence, compassion, loyalty, gentleness, politeness, humility, gratitude, humour, and tolerance. He explores the ways these concepts apply, and sometimes fail, in our everyday lives. By so doing he helps us to improve our characters, learn how to behave around others, maybe even discover what we should do with our lives.

Wisdom and Religion

Christianity and other major religions express the importance of wisdom, which they then relate to the moral virtues. Because wisdom was considered historically through the educative force of the church, many people to this day without hesitation will associate it with 'spiritual' depth and insight. But this is a mistake. If you wonder where the 'spirit' has existence, then there is no gap for it to squeeze into between the body and its mind in scientific understanding. Even if the spiritual were real, the claim to wisdom would be too narrow, since many values are not moral ones, and there is much to be wise about in this world outside the scope and interests of the churches.

Wisdom and Literature

It seems to the author that one very rich source of insights that could aid a person's development of wisdom might be to read and think about literature. The world's classics, of course, would repay anyone who takes the time in all sorts of ways. Beyond that, certain contemporary novels are particularly recommended, the ones where characters have to deal with the very kinds of situation in which the reader finds himself.

There are a few notes of caution to strike, however. Firstly, the situations and contexts of fiction rarely exactly parallel those of the reader. And if they do there is bound to be a lot of extraneous matter. Secondly, the author is presumably trying to portray life, so that some characters may behave very foolishly or in other ways fall short of the ideal in role models. And the author could, let's face it, have a poorer grasp of life than the reader.

Where you get philosophy mixed up too, as in philosophical novels like those of Iris Murdoch, there may be strange fare indeed. 'The Philosopher's Pupil' is a bleak example, providing an unstable, middle-aged male pupil as anti-hero and a philosopher with almost no human understanding, whose relationships with people, and each other, are equally disastrous and destructive. It helps in such cases to know the author's background beliefs, though the form and ideas in a novel can be much looser and more diluted than they are.

Wisdom and the Social Sciences

The English culture is very reluctant to accord mental health formal recognition because of a deep stigma and mistrust of how it will be received by others. Relatively little of the National Health Service budget is spent on mental illness, there is low emphasis on it in the medical training of doctors, and educational syllabuses in schools pay it scant regard.

Yet the inexorable rise of scientific knowledge within psychology, psychiatry, medicine, and physiology have led to much more effective treatments. Long gone are the days of electro-convulsive shock therapy and frontal brain lobotomies, for example.

It is also a profound mistake to assume that unless you have a medically diagnosed mental condition, then there is no need to bother about your mental health. There may be some lucky people who swan through life with a sunny disposition and nothing much happening to them of an adverse nature, but very few.

That being so, the rest of us would be well advised to keep our mental health sound, and build up resilience to life's potential misfortunes. One effective way to do so is to read and apply the principles in a good mental fitness guide, like that written by Butler and Hope, a clinical psychologist and consultant psychiatrist respectively (2.7).

Such a book will apply the findings of experimental research in psychology to therapeutic techniques. Typically, they will use behavioural therapies and cognitive therapy, including the interpersonal focusing on relationships. They give advice on improving skills to 'manage' your own mind, part of which is concerned with self-confidence and self-esteem. Another aspect may deal with mood swings and their control, especially in relation to anxiety and fears, as well as depression. How to avoid lifestyle dangers such as poor diet, smoking, alcohol and other drugs, lack of exercise and sleep deprivation will all contribute to overall mental wellbeing, which is a precondition of wisdom, even if it is obviously not sufficient in itself.

We may be left with a feeling that the best sources of wisdom on how to live will in fact be those books and authors that seek knowledgeably to deal with practical human problems of mental balance and interaction, namely the better members of the psychiatric and psychological professions. The author recognises that will not be a popular comment, but this is for historico-cultural reasons concerning status and stigma, rather than being a well-judged reaction.

'Self-help' books are not to be disparaged either. They can contain a mine of good sense. An example is

WISDOM

Cunningham's book, entitled 'Pure Wisdom', which has an explanatory subtitle 'The simple things that transform everyday life' (2.8). A professional personal development coach and former international athlete, he has written advice on self-improvement for ordinary people, based on what he calls the right understanding, attitudes, and practice. As might be imagined, the book draws heavily on popular psychology and situations requiring interpersonal skills.

Cunningham admits he is not really sure himself just what wisdom is, and he rightly points out that there is no consensus about it, though he claims that everybody sees it as important and worthwhile. He also (very dubiously) claims that we all have 'an intuitive understanding of what wisdom means and what it looks like.' However, even knowing something is not the same as living by it. That is the hard part, and is something developed from experience by practice, provided we have an open mind, a perspective view, tentative beliefs, and a determined willingness to change - a very tall order for most of us, sadly.

Becoming Wise

There are too many people around with unrealistic opinions of themselves who could benefit, save only that they were sufficiently self-knowing and open-minded.

A wise person would need to have a developed

understanding of human interaction, to be able to empathize with others, whilst possessing a working knowledge of how people use and exploit each other, partly as his own personal defence mechanism, sad to say.

A very great difficulty about becoming wise, even if you have the intellectual and emotional apparatus for it, is that of overcoming unhelpful and wrongful early influences in your life. People are inevitably socialised before they can reason, or have much experience, as their individuality is developing in fact, and they absorb unwittingly the social mores of their time and group. If fortunate, the influences will be mostly conducive to the later getting of wisdom. However, since few are wise, this is not very likely, and religious as well as political/class backgrounds are commonly sources of the half-baked, the prejudiced, the intolerant, the stultifying, the selfish - in fact, of all manner of malign or just plain misguided persuaders.

There is some research suggesting that older people are better at coping with life, the earlier-mentioned myth revived. MRI scans have not been able to isolate a wisdom location in the brain, but emotional and social control might improve with age, provided people absorb the lessons from their major life experiences, such as falling in love, raising a family, managing a career, dealing with failure and loss, or learn from, and reflect on, the experiences of those around them. History attests that these are very big provisos.

WISDOM

Wisdom and the Quest

In conclusion, then, the Quest here in this book is not a search for wisdom, or for happiness, emotional contentment, personal fulfilment, or social integration, notwithstanding their undoubted importance for an adjusted and mentally healthy life. The author leaves that to others who are better qualified and less troubled to say. Rather, the Quest addresses the key task of assessing what philosophy can offer to aid science in the building of a plausible, descriptive and explanatory framework of Reality. This shall be called 'worldview'. The 'ultimate human' would have to possess many fine qualities, but two of his greatest would be wisdom and worldview.

Wisdom and the Future

Finally, listen to what Maxwell has to say. He claims passionately that world universities pursue 'a seriously defective philosophy of inquiry we have inherited from the past. …. First knowledge is to be acquired, then … it can be applied to help solve social problems'(2.9). What he wants instead is a 'wisdom-inquiry' which 'gives intellectual priority to the problems that primarily need to be solved if we are to create a better world, namely problems of living - personal, social, global.' Wisdom-inquiry would include 'proposing and critically assessing possible solutions - possible actions, policies, political programmes, philosophies of life.' Maxwell dreams of 'the pursuit of knowledge and technological know-how emerging out of, and feeding back into, these fundamental intellectual activities,' And he regards 'a basic task of the university to help people discover what is genuinely of value in life and how it is to be realised.'

Maxwell admits that 'the silence is deafening' over his case for the 'urgent need for an academic revolution from knowledge to wisdom.' Certainly it seems idealistic, perhaps politically naïve, though laudable, and it fails to treat of the complex interactions that do already occur between normative and descriptive studies, which may hopefully be less polarised and antagonistic than he would have us believe.

3. APPROACHES

Introduction
History
Movements
Methods
Subjects
Topics
Problems
Syntheses
Synoptics

APPROACHES

Introduction

Because philosophy is so complex, and so unlike other academic subjects, if it is even one itself, there is no one major approach to its study such as we might commonly find. Most of the main approaches will be discussed next, therefore, and their pros and cons commented on briefly in an attempt to get a handle on what in many ways is quite weird and wonderful stuff. Is there a best approach is what we need to know.

History

It was traditional to study philosophy historically, starting possibly in the very early period, or with the Greeks, and then progressing sequentially forward in time to the present day (or usually and unhelpfully to around fifty years before, for some reason best known to academics.) The emphasis was on the famous philosophers, one by one, perhaps with some biographical details to shed light on their ideas and, only if you were lucky, an accurately sketched historical context.

Typically, the historical time frame in the Western World is divided like so (3.1):

the Ancient World	(700BC-250AD),
the Medieval World	(250-1500),
Renaissance and the Age of Reason	(1500-1750),
the Age of Revolution	(1750-1900),
the Modern World	(1900-1950),

APPROACHES

the Contemporary World   1950 to present).

The main figures in the Ancient World are the Greeks, notably Socrates, Plato, and Aristotle. The Medieval World is mainly about theology and God, St. Thomas Aquinas being prominent here.

The Renaissance is very important, partly because religious views came under challenge, and thinkers like Bacon and Leibniz presaged the scientific era. There was more emphasis on the empirical and the mathematical, one of whose originators, Descartes, is considered by some to be the founder of modern philosophy. During the Age of Revolution thought mirrored the political upheavals, producing political theorists of the calibre of Rousseau, Burke, and Bentham, Mill, and Marx. Within this period lived Kant, a giant of the subject, whose greatness is considered proportionate to the difficulty of understanding him. Although Hegel, a poor writer, possibly went further in this latter regard.

When we arrive at the Modern World, philosophy is characterized by diversity of topics and treatment more than previously. There comes to be a split between the Anglo-American analytical way of doing philosophy and the possibly less formalized, certainly more diverse, methods of the Continentals, notably the French. It is problematic to know which to mention, for who stands out rather depends on what the matter of interest is. Big names would definitely include Russell and Wittgenstein among the analytics_ Nietzsche, Heidegger, and Sartre for the Continentals.

APPROACHES

Finally, in our very brief resumé, a lot of books miss out contemporary philosophy altogether; perhaps, being charitable, we are too close in time to be sure what will last and be developed. There are also far more professional philosophers working today than ever before, so it is difficult to achieve prominence, especially as work tends to be more technical and small-scale in scope than the grand themes of the earlier days. Because their work ranged across subjects, not all whom we could name will even be regarded by everyone as philosophers - the likes of Foucault, Derrida, Rorty, Habermas might be claimed by the social sciences more widely.

A problem with historical treatments is that they can place too great an importance on individual philosophers, as distinct from the real subject-matter, namely their ideas. Philosophers can be very colourful characters in some cases. Diogenes, for example, reputedly lived in a barrel, Heidegger was allegedly a Nazi sympathiser, whilst Nietzsche went mad. Conversely, Kant was boringly metronomic in his sober habits, set in a regular domestic routine with a daily walk at the appointed hour. Spinoza modestly worked as an optical lens grinder. However, with the modern world's susceptibility to a worship of celebrity, the approach has risks as well as its undoubted human appeal. And another one is that you can end up returning again and again to the same objects of philosophical interest, as one philosopher after another follows the trail, disjointedly.

Fundamentally, when we evaluate the historical

presentation of philosophy, we see an apparently fixed 'canon' of writing which reflects, in an unexamined way, our cultural traditions. But this notion of a canon is highly questionable. Who has invented it and whom does it serve? Then again, is it really so immutable as all that? A prominent philosopher of the present day has perhaps only to make play of the fact that he was influenced particularly by such-and-such a historical figure to generate a flurry of renewed interest in that venerable philosopher and his work. This can distort the canon, as personalities within it ebb and flow in current consideration. So we get a kind of irregular, partial, and spasmodic revivalism.

Movements

Schools or movements in philosophy would often be mentioned as a possible way forward, encompassing several philosophers of note, an example being in the twentieth century with the rise of existentialism and its proponents, Heidegger and Sartre, (although some writers like Russell leave out the modern continentals as not being intellectually respectable!)

These so-called 'major' schools of philosophy have been identified and are said to include lots of 'isms'_ like scepticism, empiricism, rationalism, materialism, idealism, pragmatism_ together with a few 'ologies' like phenomenology. They are loosely accorded an historical period when they were especially influential, together with a part of the world where they flourished, a list of their main practitioners, and a characterisation of core beliefs. For instance, sceptics are inclined to doubt, empiricists deny that things can be known apart from the evidence of our senses, idealists tend to believe things are all in the mind, and so on.

There is not much difference between a 'school' and a 'philosophical movement', at any rate when the latter refers to the main period and place of influence of a school of thought. 'Movement' can also correspond to a change in the predominant way of thinking about some object, as when one school fades in influence while another rises.

One problem is that movements often encompass a variety of subjects as well as philosophy. Postmodernism is a case in point, and it has a lot to say across the whole spectrum of culture (to those gullible enough to listen).

Feminism, where practitioners work in various social and political fields, as well as the philosophical, is another movement. Their views differ markedly one from another, but all function against what they see as an unhealthy, previous male domination of their subject.(Feminism is treated at length in the author's sociology book, 'Outside the Outcrowd').

Another confusion is that a movement will do just that - move. It will come to have differing factions, and lines of development perhaps going off in different directions, such as Sartre's attempts to fuse existentialism with Marxism.

APPROACHES

There may be a more or less coherent body of central doctrines around which individual philosophers develop their own ideas, so that it can be dangerously simplistic to assume any commonality of view. Their differences are sometimes greater than the areas of agreement.

Philosophers within a given 'school' could have a manifesto for development, such as the logical positivists of the Vienna School did after the first world war, but such a 'club' approach is not typical, notably with great philosophers, who always break the mould. Sometimes, it is commentators who 'assign' philosophers to schools, without their agreement, or maybe awareness.

Movements seem to be placed in given periods of time and become a fashion of the day. What would make an enlightening study would be to assess the contextual factors concerning their coming about and passing, for they do not so much appear to have been shot down, as become tired of. Ideas to be socially influential seem to require certain qualities and vigour to enable them to persist. Cynics might say, of course, that these features may have precious little to do with their truth content.

There are additional drawbacks. For one thing these approaches can become confusingly cyclical with regard to issues. There is also a tendency to distort coverage in favour of philosophers long dead to the relative neglect of the contemporary, who at least are in a better position to know where they all went wrong. There are those, sadly, who seem to worship Plato (who was early on the scene and set many of the main questions) and they never move on, regarding him as very relevant to the new problems of our own day. There is one of the dangers of a classical education for you.

Methods

An alternative, methodological approach is rare. To start with, it might be too abstract. And there is no real consensus on the nature of the tool box either. Texts on philosophical method thus tend to be for specialists. The popular versions usually concentrate on such matters as good and bad reasoning within arguments, and would be of considerable value to most people if they applied them in any field of human endeavour as a corrective to human folly generally. Unfortunately, they are liable to be outside the curricular reach for most people at school, studying for formal qualifications as a route to the job market.

One branch of philosophical method is 'conceptual analysis', whereby the meaning and application of a term of some complexity and importance (such as 'truth', 'the good') are sharpened up by critically close examination. Unfortunately, while again such a study is likely to be enlightening for anyone, simply understanding a concept does not take us very far in dealing with the issues that might be associated with applying it in practice. And there is a tendency to confine it to language studies, whereas philosophy is more than just an exercise in semantics. To be effective, concepts have to be used in the real world, which is less perfect in form and identity, and they have to interact meaningfully with other concepts too. Concepts can strangely sometimes be used successfully in some contexts without much deep understanding of their meaning. Much everyday communication gets by on a vague use of terms. But connotations can also add a layer of complexity and a fertile ground for misunderstandings.

Subjects

Now philosophy is a meta-discipline, which is to say, it can stand outside any ordinary subjects and consider their subject-matter and methods of operation at a high level of abstraction. So each academic subject can have, potentially or actually, its own philosophy applied to the field and dealing with its own singular issues, as opposed to the core content of philosophy itself, more on which later. The approach can be very valuable to the subject practitioners, whose understanding is thereby enriched. It is also useful for those who seek a perspective across, say, a range of subjects, without too detailed an immersion in any of them. On the other hand, if you are in neither camp, it is hardly an approach that commends itself. Obviously, it does not have a lot to offer if you are not interested in the particular subjects considered either. And it does not have a substantial body of meta-philosophy as yet by which to apply the same approach to philosophy itself.

APPROACHES

Topics

The subject-based approach provides clues to an alternative way forward. Within a subject - like biology, say - there are key 'topics' of discussion, such as evolutionary theory. These can form the framework for a topic approach to philosophy. In fact, philosophy has considerably informed the discussions on evolution, be it over its relation to the theological questions of creation, or on attempts to apply Darwinism in the wider context of society, for example.

Learning from topics requires a special word of explanation, because it is not an orthodox approach or one much advocated in the introductory philosophical literature. It came to prominence in the latter part of the twentieth century in primary education, where it is still very influential. A salutary illustration will suffice, from the sciences. A topic might deal with 'forces and movement' or 'food and recipes', 'ourselves and all about me'.

A cautionary note is sounded in an article by Harlen and Holroyd.: 'The specification of the science to be taught in primary schools has thrown into sharper focus the matter of primary teachers' own understanding of the subject matter which has, for some time, been an area of concern'. In other words teaching by topics is partly advocated as a way of compensating for inadequacies in the teachers' own science education without actually giving them that education.

APPROACHES

Problems

Topics will usually be found to be too broad and vague for the purposes of philosophical analysis. They will tend to collapse into specific 'problems', such as how to resolve the attribution of biological characteristics between nature and nurture. And indeed this would seem to be the only approach worth recommending in a broad and general way, providing language does not bewitch and the problems can be accurately and appropriately phrased.

Regrettably, within every given subject, a lot of philosophical problems are liable to be generated. So when a whole spectrum of subjects is presented, the number of key problems could well be legion. There are the usual difficulties of prioritisation and selection, therefore, as a preface to any systematic undertaking of study, and the selection process will inevitably be highly complex. When you have an actual problem to work on, framing and stating it as a question can be difficult and crucial even before it is addressed.

The puzzle is - which are the problems of greatest use to study? It may be enough to start by focusing on areas of interest synoptically-in outline or summary form. The questions gradually crystallise from the melt. Building a worldview may be the right stimulus. You go for the major synoptic problems, not the obscure, technical questions, or those limited in scope. Does this give you a clear, unambiguous list? Unfortunately, not without a very subjective, value-laden process of sifting. As has been implied already, there is nothing in principle incontestable about the choices.

Syntheses

It is vital to distinguish developing a worldview from the philosophical approach known as 'synthesis', the process of combining ideas into a complex whole. The latter was popular in times before science had much advanced and philosophers would construct edifices using their powers of reasoning, rather than by observational and empirical evidence. A major instance was Hegel, who made sweeping claims about the nature of historical processes, without foundation in reality as it later transpired. There are hopeless risks involved in synthesis as an approach, but the motivation is still that of understanding the Universe, albeit there may be an underlying human aesthetic desire for it to turn out simple, coherent, unified, holistic.

Synoptics

It has already been hinted that there is a method of approaching ordinary subject knowledge almost irrespective of its content, and that is 'synoptic thinking'. As described here, it is not merely like a summary. It does not solely provide a brief outline of the field of study, but rather concentrates on its essential insights, principles, and methods.

APPROACHES

When we consider for a moment the contemporary knowledge explosion, there is certainty that few of us can come to know very much in our lifetimes. If we have formally studied at all beyond school it will probably have been only a fragment of one or just a few subject disciplines. Hence the desire of the synoptic thinker somehow to achieve what polymaths in former times apparently could, namely, a broad understanding across and of human knowledge in general terms. To attempt this at any level you would have to be ruthlessly selective, to concentrate on a few fundamental principles in each field to the exclusion of detail. A large perspective would be required at the expense of the inconsequential.

Synoptic thinking could be the way of learning to think bigger and to see interconnections as well as differences between subjects. Such people might be much sought after as communicators within and across multidisciplinary teams, solving problems that transcend traditional subject boundaries, but which are usually manned for the most part by specialists. Shallow and superficial understanding would be occupational hazards for the synoptic approach, but experts have somehow to learn to talk to each other if progress is to be made, as with multidimensional problems like climate change.

Clearly the argument is a compelling one for reforming the Educational curriculum. A synoptic approach is commended for the narrowly educated to absorb modern knowledge more widely (if they can only find the books to help them.)

APPROACHES

In his book 'Consilience', the biologist Edward Wilson uses this term title to represent 'the linking of facts and fact-based theory across disciplines to create a common groundwork of explanation'(3.2). He presumes that the real world is holistic, so that our current subject divisions are not 'reflections' of it. Instead they characterize our present, incomplete state of intellectual development.

He claims, perhaps prematurely, that the conventional subject boundaries are disappearing as we progress, being replaced by 'shifting hybrid domains' in which partial 'consilience is implicit'. Examples he provides include chemical physics and molecular genetics.

This might seem like just another word for a synoptic approach with subjects, as has already been discussed. But Wilson makes philosophical connections too in a profound statement:
'The belief in the possibility of consilience beyond science and across the other branches of learning is not yet science, but a metaphysical worldview. It cannot be proved with logic from first principles, nor grounded in any definitive set of empirical tests so far conceived. Its best support is the extrapolation of the past success of the natural sciences.'

Consilience, not surprisingly has strong critics among philosophers who resent its trespass on what they regard as their domain. They do not altogether like or trust the inexorable march of science, accusing the movement of crimes like unjustified conflation, ontological reductionism, or just plain oversimplification.

Whether they like it or not, philosophy is shrinking. The philosopher of science, Rosenberg, says more and more of it is being gobbled by the sciences, so that philosophy must now be content with just two sets of questions to answer - those that science has yet to solve, and the reasons why this has not, possibly cannot, happen.

Now with the worldview project we theoretically have a parallel to the synoptic model, but within philosophy itself, and particularly where that philosophy addresses itself to 'second-order' (meta) questions arising out of the various main academic subjects. The overview thus obtained would be at a higher level of generality still. It would draw its strands from the answers to key philosophical questions in the core problem sub-sections of philosophy. In some cases these answers will perforce be indicative rather than definite, directional rather than firmly located at a place, owing to our present, very incomplete states of enlightenment. Of course, if Rosenberg is right we may end up with a worldview where philosophical insights play second fiddle to the scientific.

Where worldviews have been written about in philosophy, and this does not seem to have occurred overmuch, they have usually been confined to religious outlooks. Whereas, to the author it seems depressingly misguided to build your framework for knowledge and belief on a completely outdated and erroneous, pre-scientific picture of the Universe. At a high level of generality, a proper worldview is needed to provide an understanding across the whole range of Reality, in place of a blind faith based on ignorance and superstition.

One word of warning about the nature of worldview: it is quite unlikely to have the appearance of being in any way simple or unified. The problem areas it will have to cover are so disparate. In principle there is no reason why the type of solution which works for one problem should also do so for another. There must be no preconceptions. Reality is likely to be very complex, but until we track it systematically across all its fields we cannot know. It's time may not be yet awhile.

White has written an intriguing book, seeking to provide a 'theory of everything'(3.3). Not the usual reductive work, which would attempt to explain the whole of science on the basis of contemporary physics, but a philosophical essay, termed 'structural-systematic', that aims to transcend physics. It can be full of radical or reactionary judgements, like his claims for the reality of aesthetic and moral values, depending on your point of view. But the holistic attempt is unusual in the modern world. By exploring a wider perspective, philosophical positions normally seen only in isolation can be subjected to more revealing tests of their veracity is the thesis. For this to have any chance, of course, its premises have to be soundly grounded, not discarded as false by most of the profession...

Likewise, Verene's 'Speculative Philosophy' looks

beyond analytical methods to let in 'the imagination of rhetorical creativity' with the aid of poetry and metaphor(3.4). It, too, is holistic, but here is a philosophy lending full scope to the artistic temperament, as opposed to the objectively scientific. No more will be said about it in the present work, except to remark as follows. If you want truth, this cannot be the way forward.

4. CORE

Introduction
Metaphysics
Logic
Epistemology
Ethics
Aesthetics
Mind
Other Subject Philosophies
Towards a New Core

CORE

Introduction

As with almost everything in philosophy, there is no complete agreement among its professional specialists as to what the essential, or 'core', subject-matter comprises. The actual picture is of a moving situation in which historical developments form a backdrop to more recent changes. Some of these are the result of fresh knowledge brought about by scientific advances. Others reflect complex cultural change. Where new subjects have emerged, philosophies have grown up around them, so that every subject might come to have its own. Likewise, modern aspects of life can be given philosophical treatments. Examples could include, say, the world of work, friendship, boredom, even. And it is fair to say that the traditional core of philosophy has been somewhat altered accordingly by more recent events. The present chapter aims to explain what and how. After all, when you look at the philosophical core it does not historically have integrity so much as being a loose affiliation of thinking disciplines.

Metaphysics

In the days of the ancient Greeks, a key branch of philosophy was 'metaphysics', a very general and ambitious discipline which sought a fundamental understanding of the underlying nature of reality itself. When this started, of course, not much was known about the Universe. Neither were there clear distinctions made between subjects in the way there are now. Later, metaphysics came to occupy the gaps between what the natural sciences had discovered and what remained unknown. Not surprisingly, many scientists (and others) questioned its legitimacy then, and they still do, preferring to wait on scientific progress for the answers, and meanwhile suspending belief. Illustrations of such metaphysical issues might include a full characterisation of the nature of time, gravity, space and the vexed theological questions, such as the possible existence and nature of God(s).

The twentieth century logical positivists did not believe there was any such thing as metaphysics in the sense of a respectable academic discipline. Here is A.J. Ayer: 'We may define a metaphysical sentence as a sentence which purports to express a genuine proposition, but does, in fact, express neither a tautology nor an empirical hypothesis. And as tautologies and empirical hypotheses form the entire class of significant propositions, we are justified in concluding that all metaphysical assertions are nonsensical' (4.1).

So metaphysics has had a contemporary history of having its status as a legitimate subject queried from time to time, but like a blob of mercury seems to ooze back out from under the thumb.

Be that as it may, there is one vexed question about metaphysics that needs to be tackled at the outset, namely its relation to 'ontology', which is sometimes regarded as one of the main branches. Ontology may be un-controversially defined as 'the study of what, if any, general classes of things exist, beyond material objects, the furniture of the Universe' (4.2). If that sounds puzzling, some of the candidates which ontologists appraise include numbers, events, properties, holes, possibilities.

So what beyond ontology is metaphysics supposed to encompass? Here is a leading practitioner, E.J. Lowe, on the question. 'It must aim, first and foremost, to elucidate certain universally applicable concepts - for example, those of identity, necessity, causation, space, and time - and then go on to examine some important doctrines which involve these concepts ... .' (4.3).

Lowe is not about to belittle his subject: 'Metaphysics ... is very arguably ineliminable and conceptually necessary as an intellectual backdrop for every other discipline. Why? Ultimately, because ... reality as a whole is unitary' and 'the central concern (of metaphysics) is with the fundamental structure of reality as a whole.' It is literally 'beyond physics'. Wait a minute, though. Does this not look suspiciously like the definition of ontology?

The feeling of the author is that the ontological issues are the ones to concentrate on within a wider metaphysics, because it could be that metaphysical discussions of concepts like time and space are inappropriate residues left after the major advances in science. These make it increasingly likely they are where any future enlightenment of the concepts belongs. Effectively, Einstein's relativity has changed the game, since the theory includes time and space and successfully explains important features of the cosmos. Similarly, causality (the study of relations between cause and effect) is being scientifically addressed in quantum mechanics these days.

Logic

Another strand to core philosophy in the beginning was 'logic', which deals with what is meant by truth thinking, and the strengths and weaknesses in reason and argument.

Much elementary traditional logic would be valuable to anybody and is today to be found in courses of critical thinking. It is also treated in methodological texts on tools of philosophical thought. More will be said later, in the relevant chapter.

Latterly much of logic can be claimed to have been moved out of philosophy altogether and into mathematics, both of which are united by deduction and something called the theory of sets. What remains inside philosophy, however, is a 'philosophy of logic', alternatively called 'philosophical logic', and this has the purpose of examining philosophically and critically, from a standpoint outside of logic itself, such matters as inference from premises to conclusions and their connections to truth. Central to these deliberations are paradoxes, where apparently reasonable assumptions lead via a trail of argument to palpably wrong conclusions. The philosophy of logic will seek to resolve such seeming contradictions, and it is a study which has mostly taken off in modern times, once other forms of logic were developed which were not subject to the rather moribund restrictions of Aristotle's syllogisms and classical logic generally.

From what has been said philosophy of logic can claim to encompass, or at least have a close connection with, the nature of mathematics. We have already seen that ontology purports to deal with the nature of numbers too.

Epistemology

A bedrock candidate to be a central part of core philosophy is 'epistemology', also called 'the theory of knowledge'. The subject, as its name suggests, seeks to discover the nature of knowledge, and to see how it differs from beliefs and opinions. It asks such sceptical questions as whether we really can know anything, and, if so, what we can know and how we could be certain that we do! Since science is the main way in which non-trivial knowledge is discovered, some philosophers regard the philosophy of science as a branch of epistemology, or perhaps the other way round. Philosophy of science will be subsumed here as a very important part of epistemology, which is taken as logically prior, since scientific knowledge does not exhaust all the knowledge we have. For example, we do have privileged knowledge of the contents of our own minds which does not depend on empirical observation.

Another problem of classification is where to place the undeniably fundamental study of the nature of truth in the scheme of things. Some philosophers would have it as a part of metaphysics; others see it in epistemology. Is the classification arbitrary, influenced by tradition, or is there a valid way of choosing? Well, metaphysics is concerned with what constitutes Reality in the most general sense and this must comprise a collection of truths. Likewise, epistemology studies the nature of knowledge, one of whose cardinal properties is that it has to be true.

Truth appears to be a requirement in assessments of some things. To that extent it is itself in principle subject to metaphysical questions about its own nature, whereas epistemology tries to deal with appraising the adequacy of criteria for knowledge, such as belief and justification, with truth taken for granted in standard treatments. Paradoxically, that might be the important clue; truth may only be a property we assign to propositions in virtue of their accordance with some aspect of Reality. Maybe the metaphysical questions about them are bogus; that is, truth is not something of itself, with an essence and analysable properties of its own, such as divisibility, for instance, as some would have it. At any rate, it is at least expedient here to deal with truth as a measure, a yardstick, the key epistemological criterion.

Ethics

A prominent area of classical philosophy was ethics; which considers the meaning and nature of terms such as 'good' and 'bad' and 'ought'. In delving into the questions of how we should live, it can quickly lead to prescriptive moral codes of behaviour and polarised discussions of morality. Nevertheless, at its best it encompasses socially useful, and politically relevant debates about new, practical dilemmas in policy, often ones emerging from scientific or technological breakthroughs, such as genetic modifications in plants and animals, including sometimes human animals.

Closely related to ethics, and a historical study of very long standing, is 'political philosophy', which inevitably looks for optimum ways of organising and controlling life in society. In so far as this dissolves, as it largely does, into value judgements of an ethical nature, the validity of its place here as an autonomous discipline is questioned.

In more recent times particularly, 'meta-ethics' has developed, a study paralleling the role of the philosophy of logic in relation to logic mentioned above. Meta-ethics seeks to consider what could possibly provide a basis for grounding ethical truth, or, indeed whether there is any such thing. It explores the nature of moral value, and whether it is subjective or objective. As with all 'meta' subjects, it stands above the discipline it is examining and is a relatively developed branch of the overarching 'meta philosophy'.

Aesthetics

Also part of classical philosophy, and a close relative of ethics, is 'aesthetics', also called 'philosophy of the arts'. The connection with ethics is that aesthetics deals with value, artistic value, so aesthetics studies that which can be said to constitute the nature of art (indeed, all the arts) and just what the meaning is of an idea like 'beauty'.

The value subjects - ethics and aesthetics - are very different from other parts of core philosophy because they are normative, not descriptive. They belong in a realm of social construction. They are not out there in nature to be discovered.

Aesthetics is very much the kind of subject which suffers from the vagaries of fashion. It perhaps reached a high-minded point in the Victorian days of John Ruskin, Oxford Professor of Fine Arts. In recent times, there has been something of a democratization arising from the spread of education in the West among the lower social classes. In consequence, and along with the liberalization of approaches, together with the increased opportunities afforded by new technologies, re-evaluation of the arts has undergone something of a revival, but with consensus more elusive than ever owing to an emergent pluralism of form and purpose in contemporary art.

Mind

Finally, and in no particular order of importance within the tradition, we come to the philosophy of mind, which exists to puzzle out the nature of the mind, how it relates to the body and brain, the nature of thinking, and consciousness itself. Originally, a key concept would have been the 'soul' and the discussions theological, or within the parameters of metaphysics. Now they are informed by contemporary developments in the science of psychology and the biology of the brain, along with medical enquiries. There is a strong hunch that the sciences will make most of the progress possible in this realm over time. Research is on a systematic footing with major breakthroughs in instrumentation to study the working brain and insights coming from multidisciplinary teams undertaking formalized experimental programmes. For example, computer models are pursued in 'cognitive psychology'. The subject of philosophy of mind is not to be confused with the philosophy of psychology, which is about the methodology of that science in the main.

Other Subject Philosophies

The twentieth century was notable for throwing up, and becoming preoccupied by various sub-subjects, such as the philosophy of language. For it came to be argued that, since most of our reasoning has perforce to use language, where logic or mathematics cannot be applied instead, then the complex nature and limitations of language as a communicating medium are fundamental to the philosophical enterprise. Philosophy is in danger of going wrong if language is not very carefully, even precisely used. Maybe a new language needs to be invented specially for it, and so forth.

CORE

Finally, there are other important subject-philosophies these days that could be considered in a broader treatment, notably the philosophy of history, a large part of which will concern historical methods and their effectiveness in tracking truth about the past.

Towards a New Core

In summary, then, there are several traditional contenders for constituent places within the core discipline of philosophy.

Looking at philosophy from a modern perspective, therefore, and recognizing that there is an inevitable element of subjective preference involved in the choice, just what can the core of philosophy reasonably be taken to constitute for the purposes of the present work?

To recap, a conventional list would be as follows:
>Metaphysics
>Epistemology
>Logic
>Ethics
>Aesthetics
>Mind.

Something of an arbitrary ragbag on the face of it, it might be said, but this is the way things went historically..

Now it is possible to classify the core branches of

philosophy into two main categories: those dealing with nature and the physical world on one hand, those concerned with the human world of culture in its broadest sense on the other. Thus we can have such dichotomous lists as:

Natural World	Human World
Metaphysics	Ethics
Epistemology	Aesthetics
Logic	Language
Mind;	History.

The author's chosen core is, however, more restricted, as was hinted earlier in the text, and with all the entries coming from the left- hand side list above, but adapted somewhat even then:

> Ontology
> Epistemology
> Philosophy of Logic
> Mind.

It is very important to understand what is being said here. This new core is the focus, along with the sciences, for an assault on Reality, knowledge of it, and the truth. Ontology has been included as the main residual focus of metaphysics; philosophy of logic, being the meta-subject, has usurped logic itself. We are not saying that realms of philosophy outside the core (and on the right hand side list) have no merit, or worse, are 'meaningless', as the logical positivists used to say of them, but they do belong firmly in the field of human constructs, the area of humanities in general terms. Of course, science is 'constructed' too, but its predictive and explanatory power, along with its technological achievements, shows it must come closer to any objective truth that may be open to humans to discover. Likewise, there will be other branches that belong on the left list, but which have been excluded from the core in partial deference to their lesser prominence in taught courses of philosophy. They include philosophy of biology and philosophy of technology. Philosophy of mathematics has been subsumed here within the philosophy of logic, with which it is very closely connected.

Another important link can thus now be formed: the philosophical core to be addressed in the book centres on the Quest, which is essentially about empirically and rationally discovering the objective realm of Reality, knowledge, truth in Nature and the Universe. Whereas the non-core, humanities-based philosophies are where people would look for wisdom about the human condition, including what to do with their knowledge of Reality, as they live their lives.

A further distinction to be reminded of is that the new core philosophy is descriptive in all its components, whereas the non-core philosophies are normative. They evaluate and make subjective judgements. Mind could then be said to have a place in both camps, but it is its scientific constitution that is of concern in the present work.

5. THINKING

Introduction
Analysis
Reason
Judgement
Explanation
Modality
Scepticism
Logical Argument
Fallacy
Popular Thinking
Irrationality
Critical Thinking
Philosophical Methods
Philosophical Tools
Conclusions

THINKING

Introduction

Philosophy has always had an aura of mystery, perhaps none more so than with regard to its methods, endlessly subject to professional disagreement as to their nature and efficacy. The present chapter's daunting task is to try and shed some light on the matter. For the purpose it will be necessary to consider elementary logic in relation to argument and to discuss popular thinking and where it can go wrong. Various important relevant concepts will be introduced and explained. No hard and fast distinction is made between philosophical methods and tools, except that methods are usually more general in scope, not narrowly applicable, technical devices. The remarks about analysis, reason, and judgement are purely of a preliminary nature at this stage of the book and will crop up again, more discursively, later.

Analysis

'Analysis' is really what philosophy consists in - the explication and application of concepts - for example, what is the 'good'? Not all philosophers agree, naturally, the modern, so-called tradition of 'analytic philosophy' being attacked by them as too limited. It is often contrasted with work by continental philosophers, notably from France, which can appear by comparison unrestrained. Look to Deleuze, Derrida, or Badiou for examples.

Schwartz is nevertheless able confidently to assert that

'analytic philosophy was the dominant Anglo-American philosophical movement of the twentieth century, and remains so today' (5.1). He explains 'the name analytic philosophy refers more to the methods than to any particular doctrine'. It 'analyses problems, concepts, issues, and arguments' by 'breaking them down into their parts, dissecting them, to find their important features. Insight comes from seeing how things….are constructed and how they can be reconstructed. Symbolic logic….remains the most distinctive tool.' It is sometimes allied to analyses of language, it uses reason, and has an affinity for scientific methods.

So it is 'reason' we turn to next, as the basis of rationality is too often taken as a given. Not surprisingly it is a minefield of problems in its own right.

Reason

Reason is a very troubling concept to philosophers precisely owing to one simple fact: it is complex to explain and define and yet it is <u>the</u> basis on which all philosophical judgements have to be made. In short, if we cannot give a satisfactory account of reason, philosophy as a project (and many other non-empirical subjects too) are completely undermined!

A common enough agreement is that reason can be a process we humans undertake in passing from stated premises or starting (axioms) to a conclusion usually via steps, the so-called 'deduction'. Reason is used in solving puzzles, in understanding ideas, in making judgements.

There are philosophical problems a plenty with reason, as has been said, notably the relation of it to emotions, whether it can be distinguished in kind as theoretical or practical, and if it has other sorts apart from deduction (and scientific 'induction' mentioned later). Again, can someone's reasoning be a cause of their action?

When people say 'the heart has its reasons' they are talking tripe, but the expression does flag up the puzzling relation between reason and emotion. Whilst rational decisions are not dominated by emotions, to what extent can/should feelings or moods be allowed to influence the thinking? Philosophers may try to be dispassionate. Ordinary folk are not so often convinced that is appropriate. And yet they are not happy with the expression of views by angry men either. So a tension potentially remains.

People can be very resistant at times to the use of reason. Why so? There are quite a few factors that can make it seem relatively unpalatable. Religious mindsets tend to be suspicious that reason can undercut faith, can demand a basis for values that are difficult to justify. If you are on the losing end of an argument you might not accept the fact and so denigrate your opponent's use of reason. If there is little trust, reason may be tainted as a cover-up for lies or true motives (as frequently seen with the bankers after the financial crisis of the late noughties). There is a view that reason, being sequential and logical, is inimical to artistic and creative thought generally. There is resistance from those who believe a great deal in intuition instead and those who place considerable store by their own subjective opinions.

Intuition is particularly troublesome, so a few remarks about it are in order at this stage. For a start, we just don't know what it is. There seems to be a vague distinction made between philosophical intuitions and ordinary ones, the former being associated with the kinds of mental states relating to beliefs, or propensities to believe. Alexander lists no fewer than five different 'conceptions' about the nature of philosophical intuitions (5.2). They range from 'opinions', to a requirement to possess 'the appearance of necessity', to abstract propositions, to where they come from, and, lastly, to those 'ratified' by philosophical reflection.

Williamson disparages intuition, along with the author, saying that we have, or need, better evidence for our philosophical conclusions (5.3). He considers intuition inessential to philosophy. And he more strongly asserts that it should not be allowed in; to do so is to invite scepticism.

Judgement

According to Baggini, reason on its own is not enough to carry an argument through, judgement also being a requirement (5.4). It does not receive the prominence accorded to logical reasoning because it cannot be put into schemes. Its only resource is rationality. There is immediately a difficulty though, because we do not have a clear view of the intimate connections between logic and rationality. Baggini naturally claims the latter subsumes, whilst going beyond, the former. The gap is filled by judgement, if there is a gap. This is no small matter, since judgement is irreplaceably fundamental to our decision-making in all fields of endeavour.

Judgement, as we know to our cost, is inclined to be poor. Some of its weaknesses stem from mediocre minds, of course, some from bias, some from a failure to consider all the evidence, or factors, some from an incorrect weighting of incommensurables..... .

Explanation

A few comments are appropriate about the role in philosophy of 'explanation' too. Nozick remarks adversely on the prevailing, exacting, modes of philosophy which seek to prove something, or at least to convince of its truth by argument. What he wants is a more modest-claiming method wherein philosophy enhances understanding, offers plausible possibilities in a spirit of the provisional, without trying to knock down rival arguments completely (5.5).

It is, predictably enough, a contested position that explanation is a legitimate philosophical goal. If it is, how does it differ from scientific explanation, especially since there is no widespread agreement even on what constitutes the latter? Scientific theories use causes or laws of nature to explain phenomena, but does philosophical explanation?

And again, is there more than one kind of philosophical explanation? Well, there might be. A candidate is conceptual analysis, where a successful analysis could be construed as a philosophical explanation (of a complex concept). Another is the functionalist account that sees philosophical explanation as answering 'why' questions (but then so does science).

In fairness, rather more would need to be said about the concept of explanation in both science and philosophy to develop clear positions, and it is a potentially fruitful topic in the philosophy of science, but outside the present purview, unfortunately. It will be noted in passing, however, that although the concept offers little in the way of problems for general conversational use in life, it may be far from the simple, primitive that its usual taking for granted seems to imply.

Modality

A useful philosophical idea is what is called 'modality', of which there are four types. Firstly, there is the world of 'actual' things. Next there are those things that have to be - the 'necessary' objects. Lastly there are 'possible' and 'impossible', those things which could exist, but don't, and those that could not. The derived concept of 'possible worlds' has kept a lot of philosophers going in recent years. It has also led to wild speculation by some theoretical physicists who postulate that all the infinite number of possible worlds actually do exist in what is not one Universe but a 'Multiverse'… . These could obey the laws of physics, whilst differing a lot or a little from the present Universe that we know and live in. The move looks like trying to solve problems by landing a whole lot more. Still, modality is a useful reminder that not all matters in logic definitely are or definitely are not. There are shades in between to contend with additionally. And whole books have been written about these so-called 'fuzzy logics'.

Scepticism

Sometimes seen as an outlook, by others as a debunking tool, 'scepticism' is a powerful position to take in any sphere of philosophy, or in arguments more widely. If progress is to be made, or even possible, the negating arguments of the sceptics will have to be dealt with. Scepticism differs in the extent to which, if at all, it lets in knowledge, but it broadly claims there is an unbridgeable gap between our starting premises and the conclusions we reach. No complete refutation of scepticism has ever been successfully given, yet it obviously has to be anathema to those who would seek or claim knowledge of absolutely anything.

THINKING

Logical Arguments

A course in formal logic is outside the scope of the present work. Nevertheless, some of its fundamentals are crucial to the conduct of truth-seeking arguments, so brief, introductory remarks are in order here. Logic is the study of the rules of argument.

'Arguments' as defined by Michales, 'are sequences of sentences or statements divided in such a way that some (the premises) are supposed to be the reason, justification or support for some other sentence in the sequence (the conclusion)' (5.6).

Arguments whose conclusions follow with certainty from their premises according to rules of inference are called 'deductive', whereas those that are more or less probable relative to their premises are called 'inductive'. Generally speaking, mathematics proceeds by deduction; science via induction, which is more open to error in principle.

Bear in mind a crucial distinction between arguments and statements (also called 'propositions'): statements can be true or false; arguments may only be 'valid' or 'invalid'. An argument is valid provided it is consistent. Hence an argument could be valid but untrue, if the conclusion logically followed by reliable steps from untrue premises. Media personages get it wrong frequently on television.

Note before we go on that there is no standard

agreement on the application of the terms 'sentence', 'statement', and 'proposition', which we have just now used. Some philosophers have made purist distinctions between them, but our treatment will say 'proposition' to stand for an expression in language of some assertion or other.

There are some very important, purely logical findings, of general application. Firstly, to 'affirm the antecedent' means to confirm the first part of a clause with the structure 'if….then'

'if p then q
p
So q.'

It is always a valid deduction.

But to affirm the consequent (the 'then' part) is erroneous. It looks like a valid argument, though, and has the form

'if p then q
q
So p.'

The astute may have noticed a symmetry here; for completion there are also 'denying the antecedent' and 'denying the consequent'. The former has the structure

'if p then q
not p
So not q.'

But the conclusion does not necessarily follow.

The latter is a valid argument, as follows:
'if p then q
not q
So not p.'

Remember again that validity is not to be confused with truth. In all these four arguments, truth will depend on the facts of the case concerning the truth or falsehood of p and q.

Other 'laws of logic' are seemingly so obvious as to be taken for granted. One is that something cannot be both p and not-p at the same time. And the 'law of the excluded middle' states that for any statement p or not-p must be true. It is fair to say this has been challenged by those philosophers who point to cases where a middle ground is claimed to exist: there are things that are neither wholly true, nor completely false. A branch of logic has grown up around such thoughts, variously called 'fuzzy logic', or the concept of 'vagueness'. There are possible links in this work to 'modality', another idea already introduced.

Fallacy

We now need to deal at this stage with the closely related concept of 'fallacy'. A fallacy is difficult to define agreeably because in popular usage it is any false proposition, whereas some philosophers will restrict it to a narrow range of errors - those of mistaking an invalid argument for a valid one, or possibly an error in argument. We have just seen two examples of logical fallacy, namely 'affirming the consequent' and 'denying the antecedent'.

There is a very influential fallacy that needs to be remedied for all our sakes, namely the one which claims that the truth about some controversial matter will always be in the middle ground. This is, of course, a political mantra among Liberal Democrats. It seems reasonable to be 'moderate' and many people will adopt this stance rather less politically as a main guide through their lives. It is easily debunked. If the truth lay half-way between A and Z, for all values of A and Z then, according to the same principle, it must also lie half-way between the half-way point between A and Z, and Z, and so on ad infinitum. But that is patently absurd.

In the wider sense, there is seemingly no end to the ways human thinking can fall into error. Informal fallacies abound. One flows from bad reasons, where conclusions are written off simply on the basis that they have been supported by poor reasons, whereas they could be true for other 'good' reasons not considered.

The 'pathetic fallacy' is the mistaken attribution of human feelings or purposes to something that is not a person, a dog perhaps. Though Flew says this is not strictly a fallacy, more a 'misconception' in his explications of the genre (5.7).

THINKING

Some fallacies have grand titles, such as 'the fallacy of Pseudo-Refuting Description'. It simply means to repudiate an idea by classifying it in an irrelevant way, such as 'boring' or 'predictable'. That does not, of course, have any power of refutation, but it can be influential nevertheless.

Then there is the 'Subject-Motive Shift', where discussion of the truth or falsity of a proposition shifts from looking at a person's evidence to regarding his motives. Hence we dismiss an argument simply because its proponent has a vested interest in its being true, whereas it still might be.

Popular Thinking

It is hard to know where informal fallacies end and other mistakes in popular thinking begin. It is important to expose a sample of the legion ways as a prelude to the more controlled thinking required of philosophers.

Arguments 'to the man' are obviously wrong, denigrating as they do people not their arguments. Most of us see through it now as a cheap political trick. As is caricature. More illustrations follow from Warburton (5.8).

The 'Straw Man' is important. People when arguing have been known to set up their opponent's position as a simple distortion of the real one, hence the 'straw man', thus making it easy to knock down. Honest philosophers, on the contrary, will ideally try to build up their opponent's position, before attacking it at the strongest points. Results of such arguments are somewhat more likely to carry weight.

Another mistake is 'black and white' thinking, when an argument is simplistically polarised as one about two extremes, when in reality there are lots of intermediate positions that could be evaluated. Classics are policy options provided to the electorate from the political left and right.

The 'slippery slope' argument is well-beloved of politicians. You observe a planned (policy) move in a direction from A to B, perhaps in itself reasonable, and argue against it on the grounds that B will then inevitably lead, perhaps via more steps, say C and D, to some obviously undesirable situation described in E. So an antidote is to attack the claim of inevitability.

A common statistical flaw is the claim that a correlation between X and Y constitutes a causal link. In fact, there may be a hidden cause, Z, or none at all, the correlation being a mere coincidence. Problems with statistics abound owing to popular ignorance of it in our largely innumerate culture. People say things like 'you can't prove anything with statistics' when they want to cast aside an argument they do not like that is statistically based. While pedantically true, exact proof is not necessary when statistics give a high mathematical probability instead, as with the connection between smoking and lung cancer. Conversely, we can too easily bandy about statistical results without knowing their origin, the size and relevance of the sample, who produced the statistics, the when, why, and how.

Michalos has a useful classification of the myriad ways in which popular thinking can go wrong apart from fallacy (5.5):

> generalization where unjustified,
> pseudo-authority used as backing,
> irrelevant appeals made,
> confusion, such as about meanings,
> and faulty classification when things
> of different kind are lumped together.

Much of the discussion about errors in popular thinking so far has disparaged politicians who, in a sense, are easy targets. But it should not be concluded that it is only, or even mostly, politicians who are to blame. We are all at it, sadly.

And one of the prominent culprits is so-called 'common sense'. Common sense is a big problem. We employ the idea all the time when we believe somebody is being stupid, saying that he lacks 'common sense'. The implication is that ordinary, right-thinking people would know better than to be like that. A lot of the talk is harmless, of course, designed to bring him to his senses. So why is it problematic?

Well, for a start it is contradictory. If the sense is that common, how could people lack it, and isn't it revealing that this happens more when we do not approve of what they are saying or doing? It also erroneously implies that something is right because believed by the great majority. But they once thought the Earth was flat.... . So common sense is not always common and not always sense. It is put forward sometimes owing to what Flew called 'an uncritical refusal to recognize complexity for what it is.'

Watts, a sociologist, flies in the face of received opinion with his 'provocative' book, claiming that common sense does a great deal of harm. He explains first, though, that 'the fragmented, inconsistent, and even self-contradictory nature of common sense does not generally present a problem in our everyday lives....(because it is) broken up into small problems, grounded in very specific contexts that we can solve more or less independently of one another. Under these circumstances, being able to connect our thought processes in a logical manner isn't really the point. It doesn't matter that absence makes the heart grow fonder in one situation, and that out of sight is out of mind in the next' (5.9). But he goes on to say that 'a quick look at history suggests that when common sense is used for purposes beyond the everyday, it can fail spectacularly.' It is 'bad at dealing with complex social phenomena' like political and economic issues.

This is because 'the combination of intuition, experience, and received wisdom on which we rely to generate common sense explanations of the social world also disguises certain errors of reasoning.' These fall into three main types, the first of which is that we give a false account of individual behaviour based on our very incomplete knowledge of them as persons. In other words, we overlook factors that are significant. Secondly, our model of collective group behaviour is very poor, owing to very incomplete knowledge of the myriad ways in which people interact. The various, largely unknown, interpersonal influences can lead to collective behaviour not predictable from the comprising individuals. The third error in common sense reasoning is that what we learn from past events is quite incomplete, lacking understanding of why they happened, and so providing a dysfunctional basis for predictions of the future.

So what we are given by common sense really is a comforting 'mythology'. The glib and ready 'explanations' of what is going on out in the world display a false assurance, the misplaced confidence to deal with our day-to-day affairs without the stark realization that most of our beliefs and understandings are very inadequate at best.

Just discussing serious issues with people is a fertile ground for illustrating the philosophical temperament in contra-distinction to others. Whyte shows other ways thoughts can turn bad (5.10).

There is the 'fallacy' of authority. We hear somebody talking authoritatively, but unless it is with the authority of knowledge as opposed to that of position, power, or plain force of personality, we should be on our guard.

When prejudices are displayed they are not always

naked. Concealment can take lots of forms, including displays of faith and reverence, efforts to rubbish sound information sources.

Where an argument should probably follow to establish the truth of a matter, philosophers would not be surprised to witness attempts to close the discussion down, or deny someone a voice.

Empty words come into play usually with emotional overlays, in favour or against, and by the deployment of jargon.

You should search for the motive behind what a person says. It is a matter of difficulty, obviously, unless we know them very well. Yet it is important enough to be decisive over the stance they take. We see it played out par excellence in almost every political debate, but it is everywhere.

Now, when folk say they are entitled to their opinion, that is correct in the democratic and nominal sense of legal rights. Unfortunately, they are also entitled to be wrong, for there is no democracy to truth. Important problems exist in society where it makes a vital difference to go along with the view best supported by evidence, whether in a minority or no.

What is very difficult to spot at times during discussions is an inconsistency in a person's position, unless it is outlandishly at odds with, say, well-known laws of nature.

THINKING

One notable kind of inconsistency is when the meaning of a word in use wanders. Another is where a value-laden conclusion is derived from entirely factual premises, a risk particularly in matters of morality. A rigid dichotomy between facts and values as belonging to different categories of thought is usually acknowledged by the analytics, but by no means all philosophers, incidentally..

'Begging the Question' is very commonplace, somehow assuming what you are trying to prove, and it is frequently used to hide an ideology. People do not want their deeply-held convictions examining. It is thus expedient to conduct the debate on a more superficial level, thereby failing to get to the heart of the matter.

Statistical arguments pose special problems for the less numerate, as has already been hinted. There is regrettably no substitute for developing your own working knowledge of the use and abuse of statistics, if you are to avoid the wool being pulled over your eyes by politicians and media pundits. You will have to learn to recognize, for instance, when a survey has been commissioned by those with a vested interest in its findings, where conclusions have been drawn from too small, or too unrepresentative a sample.

Irrationality

There are worse faults than misuse of 'common sense', of course, and other typical examples of shallow, sloppy, or otherwise inappropriate thinking. Irrationality is one of them, thus warranting a section of its own.

Irrationality is an enemy of everyone, but a cardinal sin for philosophers. It is defined in relation to the rational, where a rational thought is 'the one most likely to be correct given the information' (5.11). Not all rational thinking leads to the best outcomes. But it is irrational if someone is aware of their shortcomings of knowledge when making a decision, or deciding an action, and yet fails to look for better information, or works only with that supporting what is their predetermined belief. Self-serving bias is a frequent culprit.

It is not irrational, however, if your stance is either in ignorance or in error. Intuitions and selfish desires are poor guides though. It should be evident from this mainstream characterization that there must be vagueness about the borderline sometimes, but there are plenty of warnings available over when you are not thinking straight. Ask yourself if you are conforming out of a sense of it being expected, or if you are swayed by emotion, or too lazy to think things through, motivated by irrelevant factors like a desire to punish or reward someone, taking too big a risk, jumping to conclusions against the evidence.

A very bad form of irrationality is the colourfully named 'bullshitting'. Harry Frankfurt may, or may not, have coined the working definition of 'bullshit', but he certainly awakened philosophical interest in it. Somebody who uses bullshit a lot, is said to be one who makes statements (no doubt for his own purposes), whilst indifferent to whether or not they are true. It unfortunately deposits and smells in all sections of society, notably politics and the media, vastly expanded by amateur users of the internet.

Greenspan, an immunologist, gets to the nub: 'balanced opinions that acknowledge complex causes and competing effects are generally less effective at generating audience interest than extreme views unconstrained by inconvenient facts and designed to appeal to a predetermined demographic' (5.12). Anyone who can look objectively at the Daily Mail, instead of being brainwashed by its persistent and repetitive prejudice peddling, will know what he means. He makes the very sad observation that: 'In such an environment, truth is unlikely to be seen as a reliable, constant friend, since eventually truth proves to be inconvenient for virtually everyone.'

Critical Thinking

Obviously, is all too easy to be irrational or to commit fallacies. So intermingled with popular reasoning and entwined also with elementary logic, we have available the study of 'critical thinking', intended to be given general application as a way of improvement, and to avoid the pitfalls, possibly not mentioning any allegiance to philosophy at all.

A colourful proponent is the philosopher of mind, Daniel Dennett, who sets out a small array of very useful tools (5.13). The first of them is to be self-critical, applying the methodology not just to others, but firstly to oneself. A second piece of advice is not to alienate your potential converts, so you attempt to be as fair-minded, open to reason, and dispassionate as possible. Since most arguments you meet will be weak, don't waste your precious time exposing them. Beware using words like 'surely' to herald arguments. Nothing is to be taken as self-evident.

These are, of course, psychological strictures not philosophical tools, yet there is a symbiosis of effectiveness to be gained thereby.

Philosophical Methods

We come at long last to philosophical methods 'proper', that formal and professional arena of how the arguments are tested by those who know. It is easy to state a simple model of 'philosophical method', which goes roughly like this.

Firstly, we start by doubting the truth of something which is assumed to be the case. We question an accepted belief.

Secondly, we consider what questions to ask. It is vital here to identify the issues, so we can frame the key problems requiring solution in as clear language as we are able.

Thirdly, we devise a theory which is the attempted solution to the problem.

THINKING

And fourthly, we assemble the best arguments we can to support the theory.

We might add a fifth here, namely of anticipating critiques and bolstering any points of weakness.

Scruton sets out four major philosophical methods in outline (5.14). Whilst noting cheerfully that the search for method has occupied philosophers for centuries, a fact that should create anxiety and doubt. The first method could be called 'Rationalism', here meaning the assertion of St. Thomas Aquinas that reason rules all. Everything, including all of empirical science, is subordinate to reason, which considers the 'highest principles of all things'. It should be realized that the position originates from a time in history when the sciences were much less advanced than they are now. Religious bodies held sway and were inclined to the view that knowledge was to be found by thinking not doing (unless it was being revealed by the Divine). Whereas contemporary philosophers would surely see the role of reason as leavened by empirical findings.

The second method is 'linguistic or conceptual analysis' of words, which is really the analysis, or interpretation, of thoughts, in an attempt to uncover their meaning. It is nothing to do with syntax, the grammar of language, as such. Only then will we be in a position to try and answer the problems of philosophy, it is claimed by its acolytes. Wittgenstein even thought they could be dissolved away by such a process. Nowadays, conceptual analysis retains an important place, but only as a part of the general analytic approach which was explained at the start of the chapter. It is unlikely on its own to produce the requisite solutions to many philosophical problems, as we must after all the years of effort in the 'linguistic turn' of philosophy now suspect.

Thirdly, Scruton offers a method he calls 'critical philosophy'. The idea, due to Kant, is to look at our reasoning powers in order to ascertain their limits. In this way we will come to know 'which procedures tend towards the truth, which patterns of arguments are valid.' There may be concepts, too, that our brains cannot think without, like the space and time Kant believed were 'hardwired' in our brains.

Further explanation is probably needed here in the shape of Kant's 'transcendental' arguments. Fundamentally, such an argument shows not that some assertion is true, but that it must be assumed to be true if some sphere of thought is to be possible. Aristotle used it to say that the law of contradiction cannot be proved due to any proof requiring it, but that it must nevertheless be assumed by anyone who claims anything. There is a lot of disagreement, unfortunately, over how transcendental arguments work, what they can be used for, and what sorts there might be. It could be a cul-de-sac.

Fourth on Scruton's list there is phenomenology, 'the study of the world as it appears to consciousness'. The mind does many things, but common to all experience is what is called 'intentionality' - it is about, or directed to, things. Phenomenology is not greatly interested in the life of the mind, nor does it rely on introspection. It is the 'givenness 'of the external world that it seeks to explain. The essences of the concepts we use about the world can be seen once we have removed non-essential matters, it is claimed. Phenomenology was formerly very influential in psychology, less now we are using the methods of the physical sciences more. A significant problem with it is that there seems to be no way to convince someone who does not share the same presumed 'first-person plural' outlook. In consequence, phenomenology is rightly under powerful attack as a reliable way of reaching truths about the world.

Philosophers like to invent their own methods, needless to say. 'Dialogue' is Socrates' ancient, conversational form of argument, involving question and answer in an attempt, at least by one of the two protagonists, to clarify a matter. It suffers especially from the two flaws of being very difficult to keep focused and needing two very good minds to engage in it.

There is also Hegelian dialectic, which later influenced Marx and hence communism. Thought is said to proceed via a statement (termed a 'thesis'), followed by contradiction (called an 'antithesis'). A new starting point (called a 'synthesis') is then somehow fashioned from this opposition and the whole process probably has to repeat. However, it may be quite fanciful to try and force all reasoning into such an apparent straight jacket, even if its best exemplars could be shown to stand up to logical scrutiny, a dubious matter.

THINKING

In more recent times a fashion has grown up of performing 'thought experiments'. A thought experiment is like a scientific experiment, except that it is conducted in one's head rather than in, say, the laboratory. We think about a matter, consider its effects, then draw a conclusion, typically with a theory. These are therefore fictional experiments. In science itself, the variables would be isolated and their interactions tested, by, say, holding each one constant in turn. But in philosophy that can only happen in the imagination, and so, for this reason, some see it as an unreliable way of doing philosophy. The author regards it in principle as a constructive sign that philosophy can learn from science on occasion. The method can and should be adopted where possible, but carefully, as an adjunct to others.

Apart from thought experiments, there is a developing practice of 'experimental philosophy', wherein actual research is undertaken, much as a social scientist would do, using population surveys and the like (5.15). The aim is to provide hard data as a substitute for analysis. An illustration of the sort of thing sees a philosophical argument hinging on the truth of a premise that this is what people would think. An experiment is then framed, and a sample of people asked whether the assumption contained in the premise is well-founded or not.

Experimental Philosophy has already shone a light on the fact that our assumptions can be swayed by emotional considerations, and by our moral dispositions too. In a conversational context what is salient (or relevant) may also be a factor. Then there are questions of what is at stake, the cultural background, and gender - no doubt amongst others.

Needless to say, controversy rages among professional philosophers as to the validity of any or some experimental approaches. Philosophers could be reluctant to engage with experimental methods for an extra reason, namely that they would be taken outside their comfort zones of normal competence. Specifically, they will need quite advanced mathematical, and especially statistical, skills, which most of them will not have, and which are known to be difficult to acquire if left until adult life.

So far so not very much. Experimental philosophy after ten years or so was on the young side to convince about its likely future contributions to philosophical development, set against the thousands of years of tradition. So it remains to be seen how important it will become. Will it remain a minor, but useful, adjunct to the traditional, messy diversity of methods, or possibly come in time to dominate the subject altogether. If experimental utility is to grow, it is suspected that some practitioners will need to come from fields such the social sciences, where they can be properly trained to undertake genuine research, instead of a lay semblance of it. Cross-disciplinary ventures could prove one avenue here.

Philosophical Tools

It is very difficult to list and accurately characterize all methods of doing philosophy, as we should have realised by now. It is easier to produce a veritable catalogue of philosophical tools and techniques, though harder, and probably arbitrary to classify them into categories. Certainly there is no consensus about it. When any of those tools becomes big enough to be a 'philosophical method' in its own right can also be moot. So what follows is but a small selection of techniques, or tricks of the trade, in no particular order of importance (5.7).

A position may be proved false by demonstrating that it would lead to absurd consequences if true. This is known as the 'reductio ad absurdum'.

Analogy can be used or abused. Its applicability will depend on such factors as how closely it can model the phenomenon discussed. Particular cases can be philosophically analysed. This is part of the bigger question of metaphor and whether it is possible for us to think without and beyond it. That is a valuable study, as is the scientific tendency to develop models and simulations of some simplified aspect of reality.

Philosophers are fond of redefining a well-known concept in an unfamiliar way. Again, the tool could helpfully highlight little-known facts, or erroneously distort an argument. Watch out, too, for equivocation: a word meaning that wavers during lines of reasoning.

Philosophers sometimes grapple with circular arguments, where A obtains because B, and B obtains because A. If there is no way out, the argument is said to be 'viciously' circular. Nothing can be shown by it.

Important in philosophy are 'regresses', as they can be very destructive of theories. They, too, can be vicious. You start with some thing or process you are trying to explain, but the starting entity or process also needs explanation, and so on, to infinity. Obviously, if no way out can be found the theory becomes seen as very implausible and so no explanation at all. One such might notoriously be the problem of the 'uncaused cause', namely God. If God causes the Universe, what causes God, and so on? Naturally, not all regresses are, or need to be, infinite. But when they aren't you need to be able to explain why they are not and where they end.

Something else frequently encountered in philosophy is the vital distinction between necessary and sufficient reason. In other words, some statement may be a 'necessary' step in an argument to prove something is the case, but not in itself 'sufficient' on its own to clinch that proof without other supporting reason(s).

When considering tools, it is often important to bear in mind the limits to objectivity and the delusions of subjectivity. Philosophy is best regarded as a struggle to say something objectively true in the real world from an independent, third-person point of view. The truth is that none of us can completely remove the personal and inner mind from our accounts of what is out there. There is a spectrum extending from the completely subjective at our end to the totally objective at the other. And we have no external frame of reference to use.

Occam's Razor <u>can</u> be a useful guide. Basically, it means do not build an elaborate explanation when a simpler one would be just as effective. One suspicion about the razor, though, is that it merely introduces an unsupported aesthetic preference over how our theories should look.

Finally, be wary of the apparently 'deep' truths in case nonsense lurks below. That has frequently being alleged in philosophy, about the spectacularly opaque writings of some of its practitioners. Hegel and Heidegger spring to mind, but it is an occupational hazard for all when grappling at the limits of thought.

Conclusions

Lastly, there are a few concluding remarks to make about methods in general, whether in philosophy or in other disciplines. They can in a curious way be easier to apply than to formally characterize with exactitude. Scientists generally just proceed with their research rather than agonize about 'method' in the abstract. They pragmatically design experiments. Crucially, it should be the problem that is prior and which determines the methodology chosen and the tools applied. One suspects that method is sometimes assigned after a piece of work, instead of actually to produce it.

Great philosophers are inclined to great thoughts,

which they write about as it suits them. Nietzsche, for instance, produced a quasi-biblical, poetic work of literature in his odyssey 'Thus Spake Zarathustra.' There are more idiosyncratic approaches liable to be little adopted by other philosophers. For example, Wittgenstein's 'Tractatus' is written as a set of numbered propositions, basically forming statements, or assertions.

The long treatment of popular thinking and its pitfalls was partly drawn to demonstrate the inherently very great difficulty of doing philosophy well. When a particular fallacy or error is pointed out to us we might easily grasp it as such. Yet it is not so straightforward to avoid committing these mistakes ourselves. There are so many of them and we do not always recognize our own weaknesses and bias.

Possibly the most usual approach to doing philosophy is by precise, rational thinking with very careful use of language, examination of arguments and their consequences, for and against, framing tentative, nuanced judgements, and looking in detail at narrowly drawn, individual problems, one at a time, starting where others have left off. And that is more or less where we began the chapter!

An enormous credibility problem resides in the fact that most people will find methodology boring, howsoever it is presented. There can be no escape, no compromise, if truth is to be attained. Perhaps this in itself will sound the death-knell for a tradition of analytical philosophy in a pluralistic culture. If so, giants had better come, and bring

THINKING

with them exciting styles of discourse and expression, to say nothing of the effectiveness we are all still too patiently waiting to see…..

6. THINGS

THINGS

Introduction

As explained in chapter four, Ontology is that branch of metaphysics which is concerned in the most general sense with what things exist (6.0). Things are normally placed in one or other of the two categories - concrete and abstract. The concrete are the ordinary objects found in the Universe of space and time, things like animals, humans, non-biological entities, flora - the list is endless. The examples of concrete entities existing in space and time are called 'particulars'. Some philosophers make a distinction (of dubious worth) between particulars and 'individuals', but 'individuals' will here be regarded as meaning the same as 'particulars'. They are whatever can be counted one by one, or singled out in reference.

For this work, the concrete are not further considered as such. Nor will be traditional topics in other areas of metaphysics, including space and time. Basically the author's strong predisposition is to look for all significant insight on these concepts within the realms of the natural sciences. That better understanding has yet to come is not disputed and, it is suspected, is why their metaphysical treatments continue to thrive for the time being. Whilst we shall develop an ontology in the process of our own deliberations here, it will inevitably not be complete, although it should be explanatory of most of the main concepts and the directions of ontological truth.

THINGS

Abstracta

So what more precisely is an abstract object supposed to be? Well, it is something which obviously does not have substance as a concrete object would.

Turning to the controversies about abstract things, Effingham neatly describes four main stances. Firstly, there are those who flatly deny they exist. They would say questions about abstract things having an ontology (an existence) are quite meaningless. Second is the claim we can talk reasonably about abstract things despite their not existing. Thirdly, it is said meaningful to discuss abstract objects, but although they exist, they only do so in a trivial sense. The final position is, contrary to those above, a positive affirmation that the being of abstract things is both real and meaningful.

So which is right? The first two positions are anti-realist, whereas the second two are realist, of course. And both schools have respectable credentials. Effingham convincingly doubts position three - what we could call trivial realism - on the grounds that it is contradictory. Essentially, a property either has something in common with another property or it does not. If it does not it cannot be an example of itself.

But there is another line here, one taken by Armstrong (6.1). Abstract objects (or abstracta) are ideas that might appear indispensable, especially within science and mathematics. And whilst they do not normally exist, they do so when instantiated in the world. Armstrong rejects a strange realm of 'forms', abstract entities existing outside of space and time, such as Plato (far too influentially) believed. Though persuasive, this is not conclusive, because a programme could presumably be formulated to try and rub out all the abstracta, whilst retaining their sense. It looks a very tall order, however.

In order to make any progress with what suddenly seems a great deal more complicated, we shall explore during the chapter a small variety of abstract terms usually considered important, like facts, properties, relations, and numbers. We shall therefore suspend judgement about the ontological status of specific abstracta at this juncture, though well predisposed to Armstrong's view. First there are one or two prior questions to be disposed of.

Existence

Strawson looks at 'existence' because ontology is concerned with it at heart (6.2). A preamble about it will therefore be stated here before we go on. We may have no difficulty with the reality of rocks existing in the ordinary, conventional sense of the word 'existence'. But if we do have a problem over the existence of various abstract objects, it might be tempting to claim there is more than one mode of existence, the second or more being instanced by these abstracta. (Philosophers love to use the grandiose-sounding 'instantiated'). Strawson is matter-of-fact about it so far as 'property' or 'relation' is concerned. There is only one mode of existence. And to say a property or relation exists is merely to state that it is predicated of some object that really does exist in the Universe. The analysis looks healthy. Why should we multiply problems unnecessarily by making a false mystery over what existence means?

Nevertheless, there could be an argument, as Lowe says, over whether it is coherent to consider the existence of anything outside of space and time (6.3). But if they do exist inside, how do they? And if they don't why would the fact not undermine any reasons we may have to believe they existed?

We must have just cause to believe in things and, better still, to have knowledge of them. But if abstract objects are, so to speak, 'causally inert', as is usually claimed, they have no character by which we could come to know them, presumably.

Yet we <u>do</u> evidently seem capable of thinking about abstract objects. Of course, we can think of fictional objects too. The parallel is apt, not however exact. For fictional objects, had they existed, would have been in the spatio-temporal Universe, and they are not.

Thus the empirical evidence falls well short of answers. We must resort to reason once again.

THINGS

Universals

To deal further with abstracta we need to engage with 'universals', which have been the subject of a lot of bother in philosophy. We shall take the straightforward, traditional characterization of universals as the qualities which particular things have in common. So whilst particulars are deemed concrete, universals are said to be abstract. The term 'universal' comes about owing to the qualities or features being associated with very many objects. Lots of quite different particular objects can share the universal being rectangular, for instance.

Now, the fundamental problem for universals is do they exist? There are broadly two views and a strong divide between them.

Realists say they do exist and realism comes in two main versions. Platonic realism, as has already been hinted, envisages a separate realm of reality which abstract things, including universals, supposedly populate. But how then could they interact with the concrete real world?

Aristotle's realism, by contrast, regards the universals as existing only in their instances; as with redness exemplified by particular red things, the line Armstrong takes.

Aristotle's theory is certainly more down to earth than Plato's. We do not have a mysterious realm of existence to contend with. But it has troubles of its own, notably its failure to account for the existence of plausible universals without instances. These 'non-exemplified' universals could be so either contingently - the bombs could have gone off but didn't - or necessarily - the bombs did not go off because they were defused.

The contrary opinion, that universals do not exist, is called 'nominalism', although it is frustrating that philosophers do not even agree on usage of the term. By one version, all abstract objects are denied. According to another, universals have no existence. Since the current treatment follows tradition, and equates the abstract with the universal, we shall make no further reference to the distinction here.

Now according to nominalism, there are no universal qualities at all! All we have are particular things, which do not share a common property or attribute that could qualify as a universal. If admittedly some can resemble each other, then the resemblance will have multifold instances and be a universal. So resemblance is out, counter-intuitively, when one yellow chair looks just like another. To be a universal an entity needs to have identity, not a degree of similarity.

We need to concentrate on (anti-realist) nominalism a little more closely. Abstract entities 'are simply shadows cast by language', as Scruton puts it (6.4). And when we assert that blueness exists we are only classifying blue things under a convenient label. Ultimately these classifications, enshrined in our rules and use of language, are man-made. And they are very ingrained.

THINGS

The realist will counter-claim that the world is prior and our use of language is constrained by its reality. And, clearly, it is a danger that nominalists could run to extremes. If, instead of saying we try to track reality by our language, they maintain that we make reality ourselves using language, then they are playing God in an obvious sense. Goodman is an example of such radical nominalism (6.5).

'Conceptualism' is a variant of nominalism that explains how particulars can be universal by postulating that is the only way our minds can work. We inevitably invent conceptual frameworks of just such a structure. This is a vital consideration, for we note that even 'concepts' are abstracta and they dominate much thinking besides philosophy.

Could it be that we are deliberating over a natural mental process here - the 'abstraction' of an idea, a concept from empirical observation of a lot of cows, specific instances of 'cowness'? We might very well claim the mind has to operate thus, under Kantian constraints maybe. Yet, if so, how do we prove and account for it?

We seem to have invidious choices. Universals explain 'resemblance', yet clutter the Universe with ontological objects. Nominalism is parsimonious, but struggles with explanation. In the middle is some scheme called 'trope theory' which certainly does not reconcile the extremes, or supply an accretion of their plausible features. It is to this that we now turn in surveying the territory, because it is neither without interest nor relevance.

'Tropes', or 'modes', are said to be 'abstract particulars', though unlike abstracta they are supposed to exist in space and time, albeit only as belonging to particular concrete objects, universals being denied. Hence a hat could be green - a concrete object with a colour. For any given concrete object, of course, there will be a plethora of features, to do with size, mass, shape and so forth, these tropes being grouped together, according to 'bundle theory'.

The trouble is that further problems are thereby invoked - how and why are tropes necessarily manifested in bundles, for example? Another major difficulty for trope theory is that there will be vast numbers of objects which are green, of course, not only the hat referred to above. And yet the theory asks us to believe each instance is a unique individual, not as sense would conventionally have it, a universal entity called 'greenness'. Attempted solutions, involving devices like resemblance, appear contrived, as we have already discovered. And how can tropes plausibly have a foot in both realist and nominalist camps, given their dichotomy?

Well, at this stage we will not confuse the issues any further by exploring what are regarded here as probably inconsistent variations among nominalist theories, like the admission of some particulars as abstracta (for example, numbers, to be dealt with later).

THINGS

We proceed instead to unpack and examine main candidates for the different sorts of universal which realists believe exist. Universals are sometimes categorized as properties, relations, and kinds. All dogs allegedly exemplify the kind 'doghood'. All blue objects display the property of 'blueness'. And a relation of attraction exists between lovers. So universals are simultaneously shown by more than one object and they allegedly include the properties objects possess, the relations into which they enter, and the kinds to which they belong.

We shall start with 'kinds'.

Natural Kinds

There can be groupings of things, sometimes in order to separate them or their consideration, from other things. The purposes of classification are very varied. These can be said to be 'non-natural kinds', because if there are, for example constellations of stars grouped according to Greek myths, they will relate to human beings rather than their inherent constitutions. Sometimes referred to as 'cultural artefacts', they will not be treated further in this book.

So are there in reality 'natural kinds', where the grouping is not artificial, where the members have something fundamental in common? And where this something might well be expected to have the force of a physical law? Feasible suggestions for natural kinds could include the chemical elements. They are what Quine called

95

'logically primitive'; that is, they could not be subdivided and still remain themselves. Biological plant and animal species do not qualify, because of differences between individuals, as well as their evolutionary changes.

It is easy to see that kinds could be what science is looking for - the necessary properties of a natural kind in objective Reality. In which case our catalogue of universals will take a long time to compile. Until we have sciences at advanced states of completion we are not really going to know which are the true universals remaining, consistent with our theories, although there should be pretty firm candidates and there is no good reason why these may not be held tentatively in the meantime.

According to Scruton, we could not understand particulars unless we assigned them to 'kinds'. So kinds are arguably universals with instances. This may be too wide: natural kinds could be quite limited in scope.

Kinds do remain, for some, a metaphysical puzzle, because it may be uncertain whether in every case all members of a particular kind have an identical property, which would make them universals.

So what light does a discussion of natural kinds shed on the claim of universals to be real? We shall have to defer consideration of the question until the other supposed exemplars of universals have been examined. We turn next to 'properties'.

THINGS

Properties

A 'property' is defined, unexceptionally enough, as a quality, feature, or attribute of an object, anything or anybody. But it is regarded as distinct from the object itself and, indeed, might appear as instances in many objects. Any property that can be a feature of more than one thing is called a 'universal'.

Properties include 'colour, shape, location, temperature, mass' and the features are confined to things that exist. That is to say, a 'property' is taken to mean a 'characteristic', one which is positive, as opposed to negative. So, for instance, a door may have the property of being red, but 'not red' is no property.

Again, we will stay our ontological judgement on properties, having observed that there is probably a good deal more to be said about them, and proceed first to the third exemplar of universals, namely 'relations', which seem to have much in common with properties and, indeed, are regarded by some philosophers as aspects of them.

Relations

'Relations' are said by Loux to be universals that are shown by individual things in reference to each other, such as in kinship. Relations may be symmetrical between x and y, with x bearing a relation to y and y bearing the same to x. Cases can also be asymmetrical. Another feature is they exist in one or more places.

Now a relation seems to connect things, but how? And it is also unexplained why relations can be at all, given the truth about one thing is thereby dependent on the truth of another. Underlying scientific causality could be a way forward. Is it reasonable to postulate that relations are a more general case of property, though, and subordinate to its main analysis accordingly?

We can get into needless philosophical tangles by making dubious distinctions. When we say that D is heavier than E the relation depends on the masses of D and E. But they are both non-relational properties. So if a distinction is made that the above example is an 'external relation', not a genuine 'internal' one, we let in scepticism about the existence of external relations, and possibly internal relations too.

Others regard the distinction as important. An internal relation holds just because of the meanings of the terms. 'Nine is bigger than six' is an instance, where the relation holds between two numbers. But an external relation is exemplified by causal connections.

So we have now completed our introductory trawl through three major candidates to be classed as universals, namely- kinds, properties, and relations.

Our later conclusions will need to address both the general status of universals in ontology, together with specific verdicts on the three exemplified universal sorts discussed above.

Facts

We still have to scrutinize some other important candidates for ontological status as entities in the real world.

To the unsuspecting, and to those uninitiated into the quarrelsome ways of philosophy, we would appear to be on very safe ground with regard to 'facts'. Obviously, they are things that are the case, were the case, or will be. And in this they are in contrast to fiction. The definition would appear unremarkable and untroubled. Facts speak to the truth of some thing and can be tested by their verifiability. If they can be proven in experience, or by logical/ mathematical reason, they are facts. They are what make a proposition true. Facts are objective, they do not depend for their truth on people's opinions. And thus there cannot be any subjective facts. (But objective facts about people's subjective views obviously do exist).

Yet surprisingly, the ontology of facts is unsettled. The matter is considered by some philosophers sufficiently disturbing as to call into question the ontological status of facts altogether! Why is this?

Unfortunately, for a start, philosophers disagree whether facts are concrete or abstract. On one hand, a fact so described as something which is the case is a statement or proposition, hence an abstract entity.

On the other hand, facts are complex phenomena constituted by universals and particulars. If the proposition 'the car is yellow' is true it is a fact, and it contains a particular, 'car', together with the universal 'yellowness', which is in a relation to the car of exemplifying it. But as the proposition is a composite phenomenon and a fact then is it a universal or particular itself (or neither) since it contains both?

Furthermore, is a fact something that corresponds to a true proposition, a concrete aspect of the Universe? If the so-called 'correspondence theory of truth' is wrong, the assertion falls. And we may be back to facts being abstracta, somehow existing in the Universe, although independent of language and thought.

It may also be too hasty to conclude that facts are 'atomic entities' - indivisible, elemental truths about an aspect of the Universe. For it is obviously the case that there are composite or compound facts, not all of which reduce to simple ones. It is a fact that if it rains, the ground gets wet. But this is a more complex statement than it looks. At first glance it seems to be a composite of two elementary facts, namely that 'it rains' and 'the ground gets wet'. The complication arises owing to there being other ways for the ground to get wet than rain - a hosepipe, for instance, or water welling up from a spring.

THINGS

We must continue the analysis now with an apparently similar concept, 'states of affairs'. Armstrong (controversially) regards facts and states of affairs as synonymous.

States of Affairs

When philosophers talk of 'states of affairs' what do they talk about? A state of affairs is conventionally described as a 'situation' that exists, a way the actual world is, or one that fails to obtain. So that if we say such and such a proposition is true about the world, a state of affairs is what makes it so. Some philosophers therefore call a state of affairs a 'truth-maker' for the proposition which bears the truth. As Effingham endorses, 'states of affairs are the truth-makers for true propositions (the truth-bearers) because they will not exist unless their propositions are true'. Armstrong takes an extremist view that they constitute the complete Reality. So for him they are in space-time. His definition is: 'that thing which corresponds to an individual instantiating a particular property' (6.6). Thus each state of affairs has a particular object and a property, as with 'the battery is charged'.

On such readings states of affairs have a lot in common with facts. But are they needed in addition to them?

When we look at 'states of affairs' in an ordinary dictionary it says things like 'circumstances or condition': the word 'situation' sometimes stands in for it. There is the telling observation that it is much used in contexts where it is either imprecise or redundant. Well quite. It may be added that we use words like situation and phrases like state of affairs when it would be too time-consuming or needless to produce detailed descriptions. The usage is unremarkable and usually not remarked upon. People recognize the vague reference without any difficulty of meaning in everyday conversation and would happily acknowledge it can cover a multitude of complexities, with all sorts of contributory elements like location, surroundings, personal plight and so forth. So isn't this sort of concept just what you don't want if trying to choose suitable candidates for the furniture of the Universe? If the concept is a rag-bag and catch-all, isn't it being asked to do too much, covering and obscuring as it does so?

And aren't events like states of affairs in that regard too? We shall look at this next.

Events

'Events' are troublesome, because of their connections to other concepts mostly. They are deceptively simple to describe - as either the possession of change in property or relation of something at or for some time. Accordingly, they will have some connection with the theory of universals, as they are facts.

Doubt therefore concerns the status of events as a separate ontological category. And do events form an

102

THINGS

homogeneous or heterogeneous group? Can they have various time characteristics, from instant to enduring, can we have both the unique and the recurrent? How do they fit in with a seemingly similar concept like state of affairs?

Events have not been defined to everyone's satisfaction and theories about them abound. For starters, Kim say events have both structure and three components - an object or objects, a property, and a time or period of existence. Brand wants the last element modifying to encompass a spatial as well as temporal aspect.

Critics have camped on Kim's vagueness with regard to the numbers and sorts of property he has in mind. There is a difference, too, as to which components are essential to the given event. Does happening at a different time make it a separate event? Does happening to a different person? Kim does not say. And it is easy to draw contrary conclusions here either way.

Davidson's dual theory of events holds a spatiotemporal criterion and a causal one. Events would have to have the same cause and effect, as well as occupying the same space and time, to merge into one event.

According to Lewis, events are composed only of properties and a spatiotemporal component. However, this is insufficient to define an actual event. A further problem with the theory is that Lewis is a proponent of the existence of 'possible worlds', which adds the attendant complications concerning their controversial acceptance within Reality. We shall come to them shortly, in the section that follows.

But first let us review ordinary usage. For we consider events normally to be things that take place. We especially emphasize those social events, like weddings and sporting occasions, which are planned in advance and organised before they happen. Once again we have no problems with understanding. We can refer to events as a kind of shorthand, knowing there is much more to them than we say, and acquiescing in the undeniable complexity which arises from their compound nature. It is an irrelevance to us, something we need not bother to detail in depth. We might regard events as somehow time-limited. To illustrate, it can be blowing a gale for hours 'uneventfully', but if a tree falls over in the wind that is an 'event'.

There seems to be a complex aspect to events. They can cover vastly different phenomena with multivariate underlying causes. Thereby, they do not ideally qualify as fundamental abstract entities. In this they are similar to states of affairs. Facts look much more 'atomic' or 'elemental' than either.

So facts are maybe a better bet in the quest to find abstract existents, despite our dictionary (naively?) equating them with 'true events'.

THINGS

Possible Worlds

And are we to accord the same abstract entity status to 'possible worlds'? By the tenets of 'possible worlds' theory, there is the actual world and then there are all the other worlds that could possibly have existed, given the laws of nature, but do not. We have no need to believe that possible worlds have any ontological status in reality - something presumably beyond science to explore, and if so, not worth further sensible consideration than unicorns.

So long as we grant those non-existent possible worlds that would have obeyed scientific laws their status as 'contingently possible', we can find them useful in extending the reach of logic via modality, as we saw in the chapter on philosophical methods.

Here they are used to demonstrate the truth-conditions of propositions, as follows: true and false propositions are the ones that respectively apply or don't in the actual world. For a proposition to be possible it has to be true in at least one possible world; to be impossible it must not be able to apply in any. If a proposition is necessarily true it must be so in all possible worlds, whereas to be merely contingent there would be some possible worlds where it was true and others where it was not.

The analysis is rather neat and might give the fanciful the idea that the concept of possible worlds could be made to do so much more than is claimed for it here. Let Strawson's sentiments be recorded, counselling in favour of parsimony. The Universe is prodigiously stocked with definite real entities without conjuring any extras.

Numbers

Finally, among our candidates for existence, numbers have long been considered somewhat mysterious. They seem fundamental to reality in that we can count things we see in the world. For a lot of people they are the first (and possibly last) acquaintanceship they ever have with mathematics. And yet if numbers do exist, how do they? They would seem to be abstract entities, yet somehow in space and time. Are we not in fact just making them up for our human purposes? We shall return to the question soon.

One way of considering the problem is by using logic; specifically through the auspices of 'set theory', which will now briefly be explained. A set is in very general terms a relationship of membership, as in 'there is a set of all tigers'. A set can be made up of members with little or nothing in common. A set can be empty. Identical sets have the same members and no others. A set could have a sole member. A set may have another set or sets as members. But if we do allow this, the larger set does not also have the members of its constituent set(s) as its own members.

We may find some of these defining qualities strange, and they are in fact laid down as mathematical axioms. If we try to think of sets alternatively as 'collections' of items, then they are fairly obviously not. A collection of flora and a collection of fauna will together constitute a collection of all living things. But the set of the flora and fauna sets has only two members! Likewise, it would be odd indeed to talk of a 'collection' of none as a set, or a bunch of items with nothing in common other than arbitrarily being put into a set.

Now numbers can be reduced to sets. There is more than one way. Zermelo's reduction takes the empty set as equating to the number nought. We next build up the larger natural numbers a step at a time in logical sequence. The number one is then the set that contains the empty set - just one thing (6.7). Number two is next defined as the set which contains the empty set and the number one. And so on, each time effectively replacing a number by a set. Von Neumann's reduction comes to the same result by specifying that the successor of a number is simply the set of all its predecessors.

So to recap, we might take some large, docile animals grazing in a field. They form a set of cows, but 'set' is here perhaps not significant in itself, just a shorthand way of referring to a finite herd of real animals. These individuals are concrete, but the set of them would appear to be abstract.

You could say we have solved nothing by reducing numbers to sets. We have merely pushed the problem back to considering how sets can exist in the world as abstract entities themselves.

There is the attendant danger of asking sets to do too

much work. An understandable tendency is to try and reduce many sorts of ontological entity to sets. It is an attractive project to explain our complex world.

Properties get the treatment. Suppose a property is said to be the set of all its instances. Then, as an instance, red is the set of all red things. Easy. But, inevitably in philosophy, there are problems. Some manifest in the form of 'coextensive' properties - ones which happen to have the same instances. According to set theory their sets would have to be identical, which is not the case. So we would need to separate out exceptions.

Returning to numbers, as sets if you like, they would appear to be well-nigh indispensable to science, which is a great incentive to take a realist view of their existence, as mentioned at the outset. Quine and Putnam certainly thought so. It probably won't do for the weird ones, though, like infinity, which is riddled with uncertainty over its definition. But that is another interesting story....

Consider 'constructivism', the anti-realist theory that some entities, say numbers, depend for their existence on human invention. On the stated reading numbers would not exist without human thought. Ontologists could still claim attendant problems, nonetheless, as with what relation numbers would have to mind and, indeed, to other mental entities, including doubtless mathematical ideas more widely. It does seem rather anthropocentric to argue that mathematics is only here to help us, and in our own absence would itself be gone.

THINGS

Perhaps Armstrong has the answer. Numbers do not normally exist unless and until instantiated. So there is no such thing as number nine in the world. But it comes into existence, and in ordinary space-time, when nine ducks are swimming by on the lake. Endearing creatures apart, this is a very powerful idea, which we may with considerable profit extend to many of our concepts, mathematical and otherwise.

Conclusions

It is disappointing in the extreme to find ontology in professional disarray after so many years of effort on fundamental tasks. It does not augur well for any satisfactory outcome. The suspicion lingers that the questions are either beyond the wit of man, the wrong questions, or badly framed. Looking at the discipline today it is hard to escape its labyrinthine structure and the paucity of agreement among ontologists. The noble quest may well be futile after all.

For Ontology concerns the universe in extreme generality, and when we classify its alleged entities into separate categories, are these merely arbitrary, or functional, serving some specific purpose? And if the latter, how do we know whether the distinctions we make are fundamental? And how prove them, by dint of reason or perception, to be so? Still then, how to be certain as to the truth of whether the functions we choose are objective features inherent in the Universe, or only subjective creations of our fertile

THINGS

human minds?

Nevertheless, we have covered a lot of ground and we should try to make of it what we can in a positive vein. A huge difficulty to be faced is that philosophers can and do advance a range of alternative candidates for inclusion in their ontology, whilst denying the suitability of the ones chosen by their rivals, naturally.

Our conclusions, therefore, must inevitably be rather tentative. One way through the thicket is to start by producing a classification of putative ontological entities to show something of their independent existences. Its hierarchical nature, set out below, is a traditional one with the highest levels of generality at the top, although it does not follow the chapter's foregoing treatment, but a different one:

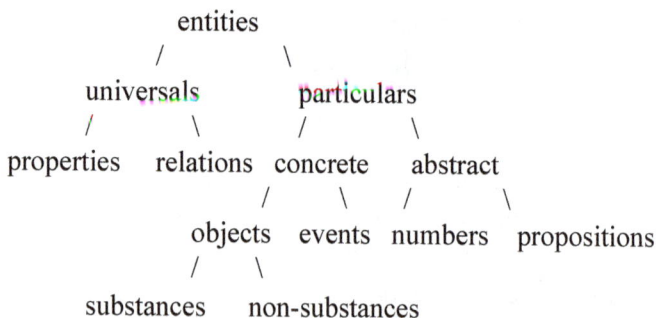

```
                    entities
                   /        \
            universals       particulars
           /        \        /          \
     properties  relations concrete    abstract
                          /    \      /        \
                     objects  events numbers  propositions
                    /      \
             substances  non-substances
```

An alternative categorization presents a different dualism at the first level of division:

THINGS

entities
/ \
concrete abstract

There is unfortunately no meeting of minds about any of this, no clinching arguments, no irrefutable evidence.

The above structures have spawned many modern versions, of which Lowe's four-category ontology is a widely-debated indicator of the field, and much criticized it has been.

Lowe's edifice has all existent entities belonging to one of four categories:

| universal kinds | universal properties |
| individual objects | individual tropes, or modes. |

In his ontology here, contrasted with his own readings of traditional structures set out above, Lowe obviously asserts that universals exist and that there is a fundamental difference between them (6.8).

The links between the four categories are said to be relations, of which there are three sorts: instantiation, characterization, and exemplification. Thus kinds are 'instantiated' by objects. Objects are 'characterized' by properties. Properties are 'exemplified' by modes. And there are other relational links too within the scheme.

Clearly Lowe's four-category ontology, incompletely

explicated here admittedly, is open to numerous avenues of potential attack. One such would be to doubt one, more, or all of the categories as being fundamental, or sceptically to dismiss the prospects for every categorical ontology of whatsoever stripe. Another line would be to question some, or each, relational link. A third questions the integrity of the sorts of relation set out here, notably whether there is a basic difference between them, as they have a tendency to look much alike to the uninitiated.

So where we can turn for enlightenment is unknown. The author will be guided in his own tentative conclusions by two main considerations.

Firstly, that we can possibly find clues, strangely enough, within our ordinary use of language. When you take a word which is rich in its meanings, and apply it in ordinary conversation in the everyday, not all people who use it will have quite the same understandings. Yet for much of the time dialogue will be quite possible between them. Now take that same word, and refine it into a concept, by stipulating a key meaning and sharpening up the area and boundaries to its applicability, and what have you got? Something that departs from common usage into the technical. When scientists do this, with say the concept of polarity in chemistry, they are looking for powerful ideas with potential for explanatory, sometimes even measurable capability.

Secondly, that which we assert, if not capable of being settled by argument or experiment, should at least be mutually consistent, and compatible with scientific principles.

Going back over the subject-matter of the chapter, therefore, we find provisionally as follows, the conclusions being set out as a series of numbered tenets. They form blunt assertions here, but are argued for, or towards, in the preceding text. Taken together, they comprise modest components of an emerging Worldview.

(1) Existence is not complex and problematic as a concept; only what exists.

(2) The distinction between concrete and abstract is practically useful and a coherent way of classifying entities. We are in time and space, so that is where the abstracta must be, not in some imaginary Platonic realm. The abstracta exist when instantiated in the world.

(3) Universals probably exist.

(4) Properties probably exist and are universals.

(5) Relations probably exist and are universals.

(6) No worthwhile distinction is made between particulars and individuals, but they are essential to the existence of universals.

(7) Natural kinds are existents and science will tell us what over time. Fundamental physical properties

like charge, and processes like energy change, may also be included.

(8) Facts are the essential, 'atomic', indivisible indicators of truth, but usually composites.

(9) Events and States of Affairs are too woolly to be useful technical concepts outside of ordinary communication. They reduce to collections of facts.

(10) Tropes or modes do not exist, as they attempt to combine incompatibles.

(11) Possible Worlds could exist in principle if, and only if, compatible with the laws discovered by science, but contingently do not in practice.

(12) Numbers are essential to ordinary mathematical and scientific usage. (Although their reduction to logical set theory can also cater for all other numbers as well as integers, it is more generally true still, as Godel proved, that mathematics cannot entirely be subsumed within logic.)

(13) Numbers exist, and in ordinary space-time, when instantiated.

(14) What is Real is what science discovers to be so. There is thus always theoretically a part of the Real beyond the known Universe. The science of limits will provide important information.

7. LOGIC

LOGIC

Introduction

There is a semantic row over whether 'philosophical logic' is exactly to be equated with 'the logic of philosophy'. Never mind. What is meant here by it is a kind of 'meta' study, wherein those concepts absolutely fundamental to rational thinking are philosophically analysed and clarified from beyond the discipline itself.. This is utterly vital if we are not to take for granted in an unlearned sort of way the relations of thought to language and how rationality links to the nature of the Universe. Note, however, that the subject is not a psychological study: it deals otherwise with the true or false characteristics of thought content. There is no generally accepted way of dividing up philosophical logic into its sub-sets, and perhaps none either concerning which are its key concepts, so the structure here will follow a mainstream contemporary group of prominent concepts: identity, reference, predication, implication, necessity, negation, probability, and mathematics in that order.

One more remark needs to be made at the outset and kept in mind throughout the chapter: in so far as language is used in logic it must always be subservient to reality. That is to say, if, by way of illustration, subject and predicate are important in the structure of sentences in language, and appear natural, we should not leap to the conclusion that reality somehow mirrors them. Just what the connections are between a line of reasoning and the real world remain to be discovered in every instance.

LOGIC

Identity

Identity should not really be controversial in the strictly logical sense, though it is obvious that applied, say, to self, the matter of what constitutes personal identity, when many features change over time, is far from easy. Anyway, it seems clear that if we do have problems in logic with identity we shall have problems with a good deal else besides. So we shall start with it.

One of the traditional 'laws of thought' is the law of identity which employs such mind-blowing formulations as 'everything is what it is' (7.1). So identity is being a single thing. Does this mean it is a relation between the thing and itself? If it is, then the matter is trivial because any statement about identity will tell us very little.

But, as hinted at above for persons, the persistence of identity over time becomes problematic when some features of the thing under consideration change. A famous illustration is 'the ship of Theseus'. The ship was preserved by replacing its decaying parts bit by bit to the original design until all was completely new. Later the old bits were reassembled and there were then two ships. So which was the original? Embedded in the meaning of the concept of identity seems to be an idea of continuity, yet the above conundrum questions in what this may consist. One tension is between its parts and the ship's design. And the problem is vastly more complex with people, of course. But this is not an attack on the integrity of the concept of identity to say we find it elusive to characterize with particular phenomena.

Now McGinn holds to four basic qualities about identity, namely that it is unitary, fundamental, indefinable, and a relation, which he defends variously (7.2). Concerning its claimed unitary nature, critics could point to prospects for different criteria of identity. Whereas what we have in fact are untold numbers of different objects, to all of which the one singular concept of identity applies.

Is identity 'indefinable'? Yes, simply because in order to define anything, identity has to be presupposed.

Is it 'fundamental'? Probably, since it is very general and it is hard to imagine anything more basic.

Finally, is it a real relation? Wittgenstein, no less, thought not. He believed no two things could be identical. McGinn disagrees, claiming a complete universality of the concept in application to all things. So woven is it into our habits of thinking that he could not countenance affairs as otherwise. But we need not trouble ourselves regarding its ontology. It is only a 'logical relation'.

The above analysis would, of course, be challengeable. Everything in philosophy is. Yet how could we find any concept simpler than this one? It would not augur well for any successful philosophical logic if we were to make a meal of it.

LOGIC

Reference

Next there is reference. Which typically deals with such matters as how 'naming words' (nouns) connect to the objects that they name.

Frege's theory heralds modern discussion. For so-called subject-predicate sentences like 'Mandy is blonde' there are two main parts: the subject, Mandy, and the predicate 'is blonde', which attributes to Mandy some property, her blondeness (7.3). 'Predicate' is clear enough, but 'subject' is ambiguous. In the sentence 'Mandy loves Marmaduke', we have two names, only one of which, Mandy, is the subject. So the names are reclassified as 'singular terms' to avoid confusion. Then 'reference' is the relation between a singular term and that object in the real world which corresponds to it, between say the names 'Marmaduke' or 'Mandy' and the persons themselves.

According to Frege, a word can only refer to something in the context of a sentence, and it makes a contribution to the reference of that sentence, which is its truth-value (whether it is true or false). This is a contemporary breakthrough in logic, or part of it (Frege's complete theory also relates reference to sense and meaning in language). One idea of import deriving is that the logical form of a sentence need not obviously be displayed by its grammatical form.

There are, needless to say, problems with reference, of which the following is a sample of the more notable (7.4).

LOGIC

Firstly, when does referring occur? I might state that Mandy is tall, but by mistake call her Tessa. If the hearer(s) realize my error, perhaps I have referred. If they do not, perhaps I have not? Does the reference have to be both accurate and understood as such to count, in other words?

Secondly, can we properly 'refer' to an object we just do not know?

Thirdly, along similar lines, can we appropriately 'refer' to things that do not exist, including the fictional, and matters of the future?

The fourth problem is the question of whether the idea of reference is even essential to language. Is it possible to dispense with it altogether?

Now, philosophers are going to accuse the writer of not taking reference seriously, by the ways in which the problems are brushed up against here. The initial observation, applicable to the first three problems, is to query what we lose if the answers are negative. Obviously the statements make sense to us, we can talk about them meaningfully, so if reference is restricted, artificially or otherwise, in its range of application, to domains where we are right, knowledgeable, talking about real things in the past or present, so what? How would we try out the problem assertions anyway?

The fourth problem is different. It could be tested in principle by doing without it and seeing if we thereby encountered insurmountable, or at least very awkward, linguistic problems. Frankly, most of us will think we have better things to do. Even if it were to be proven dispensable, it would still be too useful and 'natural seeming' to give up. Reference is an activity we carry out from the cradle on. At a very early age we point to things and when the first baby words form on our lips we are trying to name them. In any case redundancy, in the sense of there being other ways of saying or doing things, is not necessarily a fault; sometimes it is an enrichment in the language.

What we can also note, whilst philosophers refine its abstruse limits of applicability, is that reference has got to be an important concept in the semantics of language. But that is another subject altogether, outside the scope of the present work.

Predication

In a way we may seem to have already dealt with 'predication', that which is said of a subject. One philosophical question about it, though, is whether predication is merely linguistic in nature, existing as a group of words, or if it is a property that the words concerned represent. Logicians might also claim there are distinctively 'logical predicates', where a sentence is rendered in its correct logical form in some kind of meta-language for more precise use in reasoning (7.1). The last meaning will not be pursued here given the author's belief that philosophy can tolerably well proceed in natural languages without a strict need for logical form on questions of general, as opposed to very specialist, interest.

Pursuing the question first posed above, then, we need to start by elaborating briefly on the concept of predicates.

Consider the word 'blue'. It refers to the property of blueness. All objects that are blue belong to the set of blue things (7.2). So if a predicate can be true of objects, there should be a set of those objects for which that predicate is also true. Therefore, a predicate can refer to more than one object: there will be many references for it. Yet a different view of predicates would be to say they refer, not to blue objects, but to their blueness. One difference is thus that a predicate would only have one reference, not many. So what is the right answer?

The conventional view of the matter is that predication does not relate to the set or class or group of objects, but accords with the simpler idea that predicates assign properties to objects. Classes come in only when we are specifically speaking of classes.

Now looking at these positions you might be inclined to give them equal weight. If you did so, it would seem indeterminate which one was right.

However, help arrives when you consider their relative complexities. Classes will multiply them, potentially without limit; we move from one object and its (predicated) property to a large class of objects with that property.

LOGIC

So, we are trying to cope with a world in which an object will have many properties, and a property may belong to a large class of objects. Just because a property belongs to objects in a class why should we embrace class in place of it, unless to abandon the notion of property? And to do that would, arguably, present severe semantic difficulties for any scientific understanding of the Universe. We had thus better stick to predication as akin to a mathematical function, one which maps objects onto their truth values, whether true or false. In this we are with Frege, rather than Quine, who argues instead for classes.

Implication

In logic, if p implies q it cannot be that p is true and q false, but p could still be false, yet imply q. We are looking to infer the truth of one statement from another: the implication holds, when it does so, as a matter of logical fact. Note that the words inference and implication are used (as in ordinary language) synonymously. They are profoundly important, as shown by the logic of scientific discovery, of inference to the 'best' explanation on the basis of the facts.

Moore made a distinction between implication and 'entailment', with the latter being a stricter type of the former, applicable when q can be logically deduced from p. In other words, when to deny q, whilst retaining p, would be to expose a contradiction (7.1). But some have argued that entailment requires a special (unspecified) connection via meaning between p and q. That would additionally let in considerations not of a logical nature, and so muddy the waters of what is an instrumentally very useful concept. It all makes you think, though, that the processes of reasoning from firm foundations to secure conclusions are far from straightforward in all but the most glaringly obvious cases.

Necessity

In respect of modality in chapter five we noted the three positions of possible, impossible, and necessary. It is to the last of these that our attention now turns. Unremarkably, a statement is deemed 'necessary' if it must be true. Of course, necessary things could be counted as items in the larger class of the possible, but it is their particular nature we wish to consider here, restricted as usual to the logical context, as opposed, say, to the legal or factual, and to any other relevant fields of application. There would obviously be a separate study available of the relations, if any, between necessities in different disciplines, including logic.

How does McGinn proceed with this (7.2)? He postulates 'modes', logical items which are supposedly objective and real, and in which objects have properties. One such mode would be necessity, another possibility. But the epistemological question arises: how do we know whether a property is necessary, or merely possible? Metaphysically, too, what are modes and do they have an existence? These questions might be troubling, depending on one's philosophical dispositions. Fanciful conjectures as to the nature of modal entities like necessity could conceive of them as non-natural, and so capable of being dispensed with. That result would be vexing, certainly counter-intuitive for most of us ordinary mortals. But you may be asking more than is answerable directly here. Rational thought nevertheless does appear to depend on the reality of necessity and to reckon it can spot it when it applies..... .

Negation

Our final logical concept, negation, has a meaning which appears simple, unambiguous, and self-evident. It denies the truth of a statement. But as always in philosophy, problems, real or imagined, can be uncovered. Firstly, it may be worth noting the distinction which can be made between 'external' and 'internal' negation (7.1). In external negation the whole of a statement is denied, whereas only a part of the statement, or a term within it, is denied by internal negation.

Secondly, we know the 'double negative' principle: 'I don't know nothing' means 'I do know something'. This says to a logician that any statement 'implies and is implied by the negation of its negation'. Unfortunately, it leads quickly to the question of whether positive and negative statements can be identified separately, or are they just mutual negations, neither one being the negative?

You might also ask, to whatever purpose, if there is a

natural symmetry between affirming and denying? Could one be logically prior, so that it's status is more than dualistic opposition? Perhaps negation is a special, unique activity? Or maybe it could be abolished altogether? If denying is called 'negative affirming' will that do it? But if we hope not, are we being cogent? And how do we know whether the above questions, which seem rather silly to laypersons, are worthwhile in the sense of being capable of an answer?

Probability

There are unfortunately several theories about the nature of probability. The 'classical theory' is our starting point. It looks at an event and defines the probability of its occurring as a fraction (or percentage) of the total number of possibilities. So there is a one in six chance of throwing a three when a die is rolled, because the number three is only one of six numbers. The key assumption here is that all the numbers have an equal chance of coming up, and so it would seem unless the die is loaded. The troubles are at least two-fold. First, we can only apply the theory when each event is equally likely, but then we are using the concept of probability for its own analysis, or question-begging, one of the reasoning errors we outlined earlier. Second, although it has the advantage of being able to measure where it applies, how do we know that it does apply? Dice examples are simple; life is complex. There will be legion cases where the number of events is unmanageably large and anything other than equally likely.

LOGIC

So despite its popularity in school statistics classes, the classical theory is now seen to have too narrowly restricted a usefulness.

More promising is the 'frequency theory' in some ways, where probability is now defined 'as the limit of the relative frequency of a given attribute, observed in the initial part of an indefinitely long sequence of repeatable events'. The usual illustration is flipping an (unweighted) coin. The probability of heads is regarded as fifty per cent, since the coin has two sides, one of which must turn up on any given throw. Let us examine what the idea means a little more closely. If we flip the coin once we cannot tell in advance whether it will be heads or tails. So single events are beyond our prediction. If we flip it a hundred times we still cannot be sure it will come up heads half of the time. And if we flip is a thousand times, again there could be a substantial inequality between the numbers of heads and the number of tails. In short, we cannot with certainty ever decide an exact probability. We cannot 'determine' it. It makes sense only where dealing with collective events. Nevertheless, the frequency theory is empirical and objective, the normal scientific qualities. However, it fails to deal with quantum mechanics, where we cannot assign probability to a single event, such as the time for decay of a given atom in a lump of radioactive metal. Nor is it a help when outcomes cannot be predicted.

The third theory is the 'logical relation theory', making out probability to be a logical relation between the evidence and conclusion. It is thereby similar to the entailment discussed earlier, although weaker. And it would make out probability statements to be true or false. Such a relation is elusive to say the least. Moreover, it leaves 'probably q' without analysis, and could even let in subjectivism via intuition.

There are other variations, usually framed to deal with specific objections to the main theories. We shall mention only one more of these, the 'radical subjective account'. It can be as crude as you like, possibly equating the probability of an event (or state of affairs) with the strength of your belief in it. Because we can each of us be very unreliable forecasters, failed attempts have been made to bolster its credibility by requiring a 'rational' observer with a 'coherent' perspective.

Galavotti makes an interesting plea for it: 'subjective probability has an indisputable role to play in the realm of the social sciences, where personal opinions and expectations enter directly into the information used to support forecasts, forge hypotheses, and build models. Various attempts are being made to extend the use of subjective probability to the natural sciences, including quantum mechanics'.

She then summarizes the overall state of the art: 'While the controversy on the interpretation of probability is far from settled, the pluralistic approach, which avoids the temptation to force all uses of probability into a single scheme, is gaining ground'.

The author would earnestly counsel to ignore all

versions of probability theory except the frequency account and its developments, and to exercise due caution in the application of even that. Pluralism does not solve anything: it obfuscates and fails to discriminate where discrimination is due.

Mathematics

Most of the standard emphasis in the philosophy of mathematics has focused on the nature of the subject, whether real in some sense, or constructed, discovered or invented, you might say. Put that way, it is essentially a metaphysical or ontological question, whereas our focus here is on the logical. Nevertheless, it is so closely involved in the current debate about the logical connections of mathematics that brief reference probably needs to be made to it here first. Broadly, there are variants on two diametrically opposed positions - realism and anti-realism.

'Realism' is typically exemplified by Platonism. Mathematical objects and truths exist independently of human thought, in some realm of reality which is both abstract and timeless. The Platonic realm is said also to contain only perfect examples of entities, so that it would contain the perfect circle, which contrasts with all approximate versions in the ordinary world. The theory does not provide insights, however, into how there can be human knowledge of the objects in Plato's realm.

Anti-realists usually split into two main camps

LOGIC

(7.5). The first is 'intuitionism', which postulates that mathematics does not exist in the objective world; rather, it is a creation of the human mind, a very intellectual one at that. The second anti-realist school is 'formalism', whose disciples look at the abstract properties of axiom systems and how they fit together. Some see it like a kind of game, using symbols invented by mathematicians, but having no intrinsic meanings other than those assigned by their creators. So both these approaches would deny that mathematics has any kind of ontological status.

A brief resumé of supposed relations between mathematics and logic is appropriate at this stage. Russell and Whitehead famously tried to derive mathematics from logic, in a monumental work which claimed to define all mathematical objects in logical terms, using 'classes'. They also said proof in mathematics could reduce to logical proof.

A 'class' simply consists of objects or things grouped together and obviously it can have any number of members in principle from none to infinity (7.1). A class will be 'closed' if we know how many things it contains, but 'open' if the membership is infinite or alternatively indeterminate in number.

The difficulty is that, if we start with purely logical axioms, we are not able to prove the existence of classes in general. The concept of classes also leads to paradoxes, notably Russell's, whereby 'is the class of all classes that are not members of themselves a member of itself? If yes, no. If no, yes'. So classes are perhaps not the ideal starting point for a merger theory between mathematics and logic, although artificial means of diffusing Russell's paradox have been found. The theory of types does so by defining a hierarchy of different types of class, but then the concept is in danger of ambiguity as well as complexity.

All this aside, mathematical truths are usually regarded as purely rational. In other words, we deduce conclusions via inferences from starting assumptions, called axioms. We are not here dealing with physical objects and do not proceed via empirical observation. The truths are so in virtue of the meanings inherent in their concepts, not by a dependency on the outside world.

Gödel's theorem showed that any mathematical system must inevitably be incomplete. This is because of his logical demonstration that for any finite number of axioms and rules of deduction we will always be able to generate at least one true statement that can only be proved by using methods outside that system. So uncertainty could not be eradicated within mathematics, hardly then an 'edifice of truth'.

Another logical problem is that some important mathematical concepts are 'bizarre'. An example is the square root of minus one, which cannot exist (because there is no number you could square to get minus one) but which is successfully used in various physical theories, notwithstanding. If looked upon as an operator related to rotation through a right angle, it has practical application in electricity for calculations involving alternating current, for example.

A further difficulty is that some concepts, infinity being a case in point, lack coherence, but are still useful. Cantor neatly demonstrated that the concept of 'infinity', fundamental to much mathematics, is paradoxical (7.6). He defined the largest set as the set of all sets. But then you could raise the largest set to a power, and so on. Thus the idea of infinity is self-contradictory.

Now Benacerraf has produced two key questions which all philosophies of mathematics must come to terms with in modern times, namely how its objects can be referred to, and how we can have knowledge of them, given that they exist, if at all, outside the Universe of cause and effect (7.5), or so is the claim.

It may be in the fullness of time that a decisive answer to the ontological question as to the nature of mathematics will itself throw light on the above mysteries, but it is by no means certain that it will. Nor is the nature of mathematics expected to be fathomed any time soon. After all, it has been argued about for over two thousand years since the time of Plato.

What is suggested by the author as a much more manageable and potentially helpful way forward is to consider how mathematics can be so pivotal in the furtherance of scientific truth.

It is immediately problematic why mathematics can

treat of matters in the world and be the handmaiden of much scientific endeavour. Falsely referred to long ago as 'the queen of the sciences', mathematics is nonetheless the 'language' of choice of the sciences, one of its ideals being to frame theoretical principles in numerical laws and algebraic equations.

Quine's view would seem defeatist here. He said that owing to the use of mathematics and logic to relate empirical evidence to the rest of science they were both inextricably woven into its whole fabric.

Others, like Field, have challenged Quine's position, claiming an easy possible separation. According to Field, who is an 'anti-realist' about mathematics, science can be conducted entirely without it. We might add that it often is, and not just in fledgling sciences either. Field, though, does concede that mathematics is useful in science and is a 'convenient shortcut'.

Putnam disagrees. He uses the indispensability argument to counter from a realist perspective that, because mathematics is involved in the expression of physical theory, the existence of mathematical objects must also be accepted. We saw in the chapter on Ontology that Armstrong has a neat way round this.

Körner's opinion also attempts to diffuse the controversy: 'mathematical concepts describe neither a super-empirical reality, an inter-subjective intuition, nor indeed, sense experience, and the connection of a mathematical theory with sense experience consists in the identification, within certain contexts and for certain purposes, of mathematical with empirical concepts' (7.7). His claim is more modest than either of its stark alternatives. And it could well be formulated as a research programme to test it out in the detail. The author regards it as the plausible way forward accordingly.

Barrow has done some relevant preparatory work. He provides a useful list of abstract branches of mathematics applicable to the world (7.8). Conics is well known for its uses in geometrical topics, such as the elliptical laws of planetary motion discovered by Kepler. Non-Euclidean geometries have been utilized to describe with accuracy gravitational distortions of space-time. And group theory, a systematic study of symmetry, with its operations such as rotation, has been applied to molecular motion and optical isomerism. Even in the popular imagination nowadays, there is an awareness of chaos theory and the exotic Mandelbrot patterns, but it is less well realized that its non-linear equations provide a breakthrough in the understanding of turbulent motions in fluids.

Take geometry. As conventionally taught it is essentially that discovered by Euclid, an ancient Greek. And it is generally assumed to fit the world. After all, we can use it for calculating crucial factors like angles without which, among many other horrors, buildings would fall down more often than they do. Yet if you change some of the axioms in Euclid's geometry, breaking his rules in the process, you can develop other geometrical systems under different rules, such as that of Riemann. But lo and behold, they give results which also have their usages, such as in the accurate description of the elliptical and hyperbolic features of space-time, which Einstein's relativity showed was curved owing to gravitational mass. Draw a triangle on a balloon, then blow it up. You will be able to see for yourself that Euclid's stricture on the three interior angles adding up to one hundred and eighty degrees only applies to a flat, two-dimensional surface.

When we look at the development of mathematics we can see some pretty moribund topics, like the geometry of elementary shapes (7.9). But new areas are still being 'generated' after a history of thousands of years, showing an internal capacity which has not reached exhaustion even now. There is a dynamic interplay between science, its technological needs, and new mathematics perhaps designed for specific practical purposes. There would thus appear to be a symbiotic creative aspect worthy of study.

Barrow develops a line of thought to point out features of the world which aid its understanding by mathematical methods. Fundamental is linearity, which is quantitatively characterized by numerical equations, and for which the whole is the sum of its parts, making for ease of calculation. Symmetry has already been mentioned. There also appears to be a continuity in nature such that changes are well tracked by differential equations. And the principle of extrapolation relies on the 'global' being somewhat like the 'local', only bigger.

LOGIC

These comparators are highly involved and very specific, but across the whole vast field a mapping of interactions is capable of being undertaken. When it is reasonably comprehensive, we may ask again as to the connections of mathematics and its internal logics to the world. Its manifold particular instances might baulk the generality of answer so beloved of philosophers, though.

The strong hunch here is that the results of the research programme suggested would bolster an anti-realist picture of mathematics (not at all inconsistent with a realist notion of science, by the way). And that the constructivist view emerging will turn its back on intuitionism without embracing formalism either.

8. KNOWLEDGE

Introduction
Types of Knowledge
Sources of Knowledge
      (i)   A priori
      (ii)   Perception
      (iii)   Introspection
      (iv)   Memory
      (v)   Society
      (vi)   Testimony
The Nature of Knowledge
      (i)   Definition
      (ii)   Belief
      (iii)   Justification
      (iv)   Truth
The Architectural Structure of Knowledge
Barriers to Knowledge
Scepticism
Conclusions

KNOWLEDGE

Introduction

'Epistemology', or 'The Theory of Knowledge', is the subject-matter of the present chapter. Broadly, it asks questions like 'what is it to 'know' something?' And how is knowledge related to other concepts in its family, such as truth, belief, evidence, and justification?

Again, to folk not versed in philosophy, questions like these will probably seem at first acquaintance banal, puerile even. Aren't the answers obvious? Well, we certainly usually behave as though they are. And in the matters of practical, everyday living there is much which we just must take on trust, having neither the time, the resources, (nor usually the interest, it has to be said) to dig underneath the surface.

So the current chapter will aim to supply a brief and modest corrective to this pragmatic approach. 'Modest' only, for as usual in philosophy, the problems soon prove surprisingly difficult, and consensus among the professionals is hard to find. Yet in the modern scientific world, as metaphysics yields more of its ground, epistemology could reasonably lay claim to being even the core field in contemporary philosophy today.

We shall start by looking at the types of knowledge and where knowledge is acquired - its sources - before venturing to say in detail what knowledge is. We proceed, in other words, from a standard view to matters which are much more contentious regarding the nature of knowledge itself, including sceptical views as to whether there is even any such thing.

Types of Knowledge

There are various classifications here. One, due to Ryle, is to distinguish 'knowing how' from 'knowing that' (8.1). In other words, know-how is commonly used of skills, like riding a bicycle or swimming. Typically these are action-based, whereas knowing that refers to propositions or facts. 'He knew that something was the case'. This is a useful approach and may take in objects in the world generally.

What may be disconcerting is that the classifications tend to be dualisms. They make a particular contrast between the two possibilities instead of comprehensively categorizing types of knowledge in an integrated way.

Another illustration is unsatisfactory for a further reason too in depending on understanding of a certain theory. This is Russell's dualism of 'knowledge by acquaintance' and 'knowledge by description'. The former seems to have connotations of the personal and immediate, but is not precisely drawn. The latter is where there is no personal acquaintance, but we get the knowledge second-hand.

It should be noticed by now that there are no 'pure' types of knowledge in that we classify them by such references as how we obtain them rather than what they inherently are.

KNOWLEDGE

A good example is the dualism, 'a priori knowledge' and "empirical' or 'aposteriori' knowledge', the former being knowledge we can have without the need, as with the latter, for perceptual evidence. Typically, a priori knowledge is cited in logical and mathematical truths. The concept has all sorts of problems, some of which we will encounter later.

The hope for a taxonomy of knowledge types will be left here for the moment, but it looks messy in prospect.

Sources of Knowledge.

It is much easier, fortunately, to list and characterize the sources from which we obtain our knowledge. The account that follows needs to be critical, however, for there is much to go wrong in the process.

The first target is 'intuition', popularly believed to be a reliable source of knowledge. We have a 'hunch' that something is the case. In definitional terms, there is a relation between an object in the world and our mind, with the emphasis being on this as 'direct', with minimal contribution from the mind by way of reflection on the matter. So-called 'common sense', which we discussed in chapter five, is often of this nature. Intuition was disparaged in that chapter in the section on reason, which it is the antithesis of.

Among the candidates for knowledge found by

intuition have variously been moral concepts, like 'good' and 'right', mathematical and logical truths, introspective notions like features of our personal identity, knowledge garnered via the senses. Characteristically, philosophers argue about what is to be included in the list. Many deny any and all. Cases may be asserted by philosophers to exist whereby there are no reasons to be found in support of some 'truth', and no way to verify it either. The author is with Hume in wanting 'to commit to the flames' any such conclusions for which we can adduce neither rational argument, nor evidence.

(i) A Priori

Standard treatments (usefully) state that there is such a thing as a priori knowledge. It is said to be had in proposition p when we realise it is necessarily true.

'A priori' knowledge, so called, is that which we do not need any evidence for. It comes instead from our powers of reasoning. There are different ways, some say, that this can be so. For example, a truth such as 'all bachelors are unmarried' is 'analytic'. That is to say, it is true in virtue of the meaning of the words used in the proposition. Logical truths are of this type, involving valid arguments like: 'p or q, not q, therefore p'. The deduction leads reliably from true premises which are self-evident axioms, via a step, or steps, to a true conclusion. Much in mathematics is also true in the same way, such as '2+2 = 4'.

KNOWLEDGE

Now, disagreements occur over whether we can call all a priori truths 'necessary'. We know the reverse is not the case, presumably because we can have necessary truths which require perceptual evidence. The opposite of 'necessary' is contingent, so we have a parallel with the a priori empirical dualism.

Add in the other dualistic parallel, between the 'analytic' and the 'synthetic' propositions in logic, and we have the propensity for a lot of trouble. (We recall that synthetic propositions do not have the sense of the subject contained in their predicate).

The trouble arises when various philosophers try to create splits within the various distinctions, such as Kant's 'synthetic a priori.' The hunch of the present author is that the avenues will not prove particularly fruitful to explore.

Devitt is not alone as a philosopher who even denies the existence of the a priori altogether, essentially by claiming that simple a priori 'truths' have to face the 'tribunal of experience', but not individually, only as part of a system. Moreover, he says the notion of rational insight as a source of knowledge is nebulous. On this interpretation, of course, any truths whatever may be held only tentatively, as better enlightenment can always in principle necessitate further revisions.

KNOWLEDGE

(ii) Perception

The next and main source of knowledge is perception. Through our senses we perceive the world. The basis of this perception comes to formulate many beliefs and acquire a great deal of knowledge. Now the fact that perception provides us with the experience to ground knowledge is not open to serious doubt (unless you are an extreme sceptic). Broadly it consists of four essential parts: the person doing the seeing, hearing, feeling, smelling, and tasting; the object(s) in the world; the sensory experience itself; and the causal link between the object and the perceiver (8.2).

There are theories to explain perception, of which main ones include realism that what is perceived is both real and out there, or it is just appearance, whereby all we perceive we are unable to get behind, so we don't know whether the objects have an inner character that does not show. 'Sense data' theories claim we can only experience reality indirectly, via sense data which are their manifest representatives.

Under adverbial theories, the object produces a sensory experience of itself in the perceiver, whereas phenomenalism has it the other way about: it is the perceiver who constructs the external objects, in one notable version from the raw material of the sense data.

It seems quite plausible that science will in time be able to discriminate among the theories in truth terms and it is reasonable to leave the matter in their hands until it does.

KNOWLEDGE

There are many unknowns left in perception to investigate, dyslexia for one, and which may not perhaps all yield to knowledge. Yet there is nothing in the philosophical accounts we have seen to be especially helpful to the scientific enterprise. Indeed, some of them are quite negative over the prospects..

(iii) Introspection

This term needs very careful consideration as it can lead over precipices. If we 'introspect' - look inside our own mind - we can form very clear and direct beliefs about what is happening there. This feat of self-consciousness goes on all the time we are awake and beliefs so obtained are usually true, thereby constituting knowledge. Yet such beliefs are not infallible. And whilst we normally have justification for holding them we sometimes do not. So we cannot conclude, as Descartes did, that introspected beliefs are a foundation for the whole of knowledge. The key question will be how far this internal access can take us towards what would be 'privileged' knowledge.

The popular belief that 'we know our own minds' has only narrow currency in relation to facts of the outside world. Many people suffer from mental illnesses, in part because they find their own psychological states a subject of confusion, let alone control.

What may need clarification about introspection is that it can generate both personal internal 'a priori' knowledge, and also empirical knowledge when we react to external objects and events by thinking about them.

(iv) Memory

That memory is a source of knowledge is unexceptional, though it serves in the secondary role of recall rather than origination. There are close links, obviously, between memory and the more fundamental perception, for it salvages much important information acquired via our senses. One large set of problems for philosophers here is that memory is something of a challenge to psychology. We all know, also, that it can notoriously play tricks.

As a major source of our beliefs, memory must be causally linked, yet it is hard to see how. Naïve realism falsely claims we remember things exactly as they are and has no theory to explain forgetting. Other theories tend to rely on mental images being formulated, but in the remembrance of an event sometimes they are and sometimes they are not.

Epistemologically, of course, the key importance of memory is that it entails our having knowledge in cases where the propositions we remember happen to be true. So long as we tread cautiously, in full awareness of memory's limitations, we might possibly use it (we do anyway) as a legitimate source of knowledge.

Yet, since it is so unreliable it would be far preferable

to take memorial evidence in conjunction with some independent grounds, if such exist, or can be obtained. If not, it would usually be better to suspend any judgement claiming knowledge, even if our convictions are strong enough to hold to a belief.

(v) Society

Goldman seeks to add 'social epistemology' to the traditional theory of knowledge (8.3). But what is it? Does it have the same subject matter, but covered from a social rather than individual perspective, perhaps, or is its agenda genuinely different? Will one transcend the other, or are they coterminous? How would such a study relate to, and be separated from, the sociology of knowledge?

As usual, there is no agreement on the answers, but Goldman himself, as the present author, defends the key concepts of traditional epistemology, such as knowledge, truth, and justification. You can also continue to have individuals as the agents or subject, whilst emphasizing the influential importance of institutions and relations among social groups, short of endowing them with epistemic properties of their own.

There is plenty of scope for radicals here, of course, but the strong version of social constructivism, whereby entities ostensibly in the world are actually socially constructed as opposed to discovered, need not be adopted. The moderate view behind weak versions is that only our representations of objects in the world are constructed, or modelled, if you like, but we do not reify them into existence. They are there already, and it is our descriptions and explanations that are approximate when 'true'.

There are no doubt many plausible approaches to the use of social epistemology. One such is 'doxology'. Goldman defines the subject of doxology widely as 'any account or theory of belief - formation and transmission', whereas it is commonly used narrowly in religious contexts. He sees it as helpful to epistemology because it can clarify paths and production processes for beliefs. Unfortunately, this also includes the wrong ones as well as true beliefs, but since most human beliefs are generated via social intercourse, epistemology can then, at least in principle, evaluate the relative effectiveness of social routes in producing genuine knowledge.

Another of the possible routes for the social communication of knowledge is said by some to be through units of culture called 'memes'. Invented by the geneticist, Richard Dawkins, the term covers much else besides the vehicle of ideas we discuss here, such as tunes, fashions, and so on. By some mechanism paralleling the biological transmission of genes, postulated but not really evidenced, the ideas are passed on - replicated, so to speak. If something gets copied the theory is not (yet?) good enough to predict what and explain how. There are those claiming imitation as a factor, others look to influence leading to transformations or alterations, rather than strict formation of replicas. At any rate, there is quite a way to go before we can accept memetic approaches as credible aids to understanding, not just a seductive analogy with the way the biology of our genes functions down the generations.

But could there be social conditions that promoted truth over falsehood, acted (analogously) as an attractor for truth? The proposition does seem dubious given the high scale and frequency of folly observed in most communities. One bugbear is that propositions are often difficult to disprove. They can some of them in the meantime acquire popular support.

Concerning the public domain, the social methods of acquiring knowledge should be fruitful areas for social epistemologists to study if they can get over ideologies. Because of the knowledge explosion, nobody has all the expertise necessary even to answer the practical questions of everyday life these days. So we have to help each other, with all the uncertainty and lack of reliability that entails.

Finally, where we can make great use of social philosophy, Goldman thinks, is in assessing the positive and negative effects of the various social practices on the prospects for acquiring true belief. Some are screamingly obvious, of course, without the pretensions of formal study. You would not, for instance, seek an objective evaluation of the worth of referees in a football crowd at the match. Yet others are more subtle. And if not that then sinister in their lack of transparency publically complained about within the organs of government and commercial institutions. One area where study could already be bearing fruit across society for those willing to listen is in the general and specific appraisals of the roles, performances and influence of experts. It is therefore to testimony that we next turn our attention.

(vi) Testimony

Testimony, as we have seen, is one of the indirect sources of belief, and thereby, hopefully of knowledge too. But testimony is notoriously unreliable, as we may have noted from many a controversial court case verdict. Archetypically, how does the relatively ignorant lay man successfully evaluate the testimony of an expert witness? It is far from evident how he should proceed. And the situation is clouded still further if on a jury he has to hear the conflicting testimony of two expert witnesses. Obviously the picture is a stereotypical one; in reality there will be degrees of expertise and ignorance.

A main need is to address the nature of expertise in the putative expert and question it. There will presumably be partial safeguards through formal credentials like academic and professional qualifications, years of relevant and well-regarded practitioner experience and the like (notwithstanding its subjective elements). But even the intelligent layman is really in a weak position to evaluate the worth of all this, any more than the testimony he hears from him. So what can he do? In a court of law probably not a lot so hidebound will he be with procedural and role constraints.

However, testimony is not confined to legal matters. Outside, if he had the time, expertise, and the resources, he could look at the arguments and evidence the experts adduce, how they support their position, how they criticize others. He could be swayed if the experts agree. He could look at how the experts have (reportedly) performed in the past in similar situations, and he could mull over their stated interests, and apparent biases, perhaps, as well as who may be paying them.

Of course, there may be better arguments and evidence on one or the other side, or both, which the present experts do not draw out. Neither is their consensus any indication, of itself, that they speak the truth. Taken together, all these avenues may have a partial traction. Cumulatively, however, they offer no guarantees whatsoever.

The Nature of Knowledge

We have thus now seen that the sources of knowledge are various and not always reliable. but in seeking 'knowledge', what is it we are looking for?

(i) Definition

There is a standard, very well-known approach to the definition of knowledge that runs as follows (8.4). We think that knowledge is something like belief, except that the latter can be either true or false, whereas knowledge cannot, of course, be anything other than true. So we proceed to define our view and tentatively suggest that knowledge is 'true belief'. Wait though, you may have no reason for holding a particular belief, which could still happen to be true nevertheless. So we might now want to qualify our characterization of knowledge as 'justified true belief'.

This looks much better, except that Gettier came along and set up a whole series of counter examples to show its inadequacy (8.5). The essence of any Gettier case is that the scenario shows someone with a justified true belief who still lacks knowledge of that belief because the belief was obtained by luck. An example would be somebody looking at a clock he was unaware was stopped, but which so happened to be at the right time.

In reaction to Gettier counter examples, Audi fell back on the softer assertion that:
'Knowledge is true belief based in the right way on the right kind of ground'. The definition is disappointingly subjective and it begs the questions of what the vague terms 'right', 'way', and 'ground' mean in this context.

Gettier spawned a huge literature seeking to find a way to a flawless definition of knowledge. No-one has succeeded yet, and he wisely did not join the debate.

This is not to suggest there is nothing sensible or useful about our working definition of knowledge as justified true belief, and it may well be applicable across the wide ranges.

KNOWLEDGE

To look at each element in turn is instructive and insightful, so that will be next.

(ii) Belief

An authoritative basic treatment of belief suggests it is similar to knowledge in the distinct sources from which it can stem.. These are perception (we believe something on the evidence of our senses of sight, smell, hearing, and touch) - memory of the past-introspection (where we look inside our mind) - and the 'a priori' (where only reason is applied). The four sources are direct ones. There are indirect ones too, notably induction and testimony. The former is based on our previous experiences, whereas the latter relies on evidence given to us by other people.

Sadly, it has to be added that we also have irrational belief. This could be in fairies, or absolutely anything, however half-baked or cogent. It is marked by not coming from any of the characteristic sources of belief which might have the potential for promoting it to the standing of actual knowledge.

But before a belief can become knowledge it has to possess further characteristics, pass certain tests.

(iii) Justification

We have seen that judgement plays a key role in the

KNOWLEDGE

'traditional' modern definition of knowledge as 'justified true belief'. Here we will unpack it a little.

Perhaps the first point to mention is the hierarchy arguments about the relative importance and primacy of epistemic concepts (8.6). Judgement is one candidate for the accolade of first importance, more so even than knowledge itself, because in coming to our beliefs, we properly should employ justification arguments and evidence of one kind or another. It is little good just having a sort of feeling about things.

We sometimes claim to know something 'intuitively', and may attempt to justify it by an appeal to 'common sense'. All manner of things are said to be known in this way, from objects to truths. The key characteristic of intuition is directness between the insight and the mind, with no influence of thought which could engender interpretations.

Naturally disputed, it is probably on safest ground when talking about our inner selves. Pre-rational, it may amount to knowledge we cannot account for which stems from our subconscious. That could yield to investigation, or perhaps not.

But there are also worrying cases, interesting to philosophy, and commonplace in ethics among others, in which it is asserted there are no reasons to be discovered, nor means of ascertaining their truth either. The present author would strongly dispute that intuitions as vague and tenuously supported as these should be acceptable, but he cannot deny their pervasive popular influence and apparent respectability in contemporary thought.

Reason plays a decisive part in vast numbers of judgements. From given or obtained information we infer some claim to knowledge or other. The processes of 'inference' are broadly of two sorts - using deduction or induction.

The former is the domain of logical argument. The inference is from starting points, taken as already known, via correct reasoning to true conclusions.

It is possible to attack almost any position, as we now realize, and the following is disconcerting if allowable. For example, if you know that p is true, and you also correctly deduce that p guarantees the truth of q, then you know that q is true. But do you? Some, like Dretske, would say not necessarily, and they put up alleged counter- examples to bolster their case.

How we infer the truth of one belief on the basis of another, or others, is not straightforward. We can proceed using poor reasoning for one thing and lose our way. Inference also has two components - the inferential process and its content. Working backwards, we cannot tell by looking at a proposition whether it is believed following a process of inference, or by some alternative means. Historically, we might later even forget that inference was involved at all.

KNOWLEDGE

It is important to note that inference is not a basic source of either justification or knowledge. Rather, it transmits and extends them, requiring premises before it can start.

In our exploration of judgement, we will next consider what should on the face of it be easy - to compare similar things (8.6). The complication is that an object or process can have many features. Comparisons of similarity then have to be assessed in arbitrarily different ways depending on which features are chosen as the relevant attributes. It is but a small step from here to classification and its attendant categorizations. That way lies difficulty, especially when you realize that not all boundaries between categories will be clear-cut. This is where a lot of us go wrong. For we tend to think all boundaries should be sharp, with membership of each category definite in number and certain in assignment, whereas Reality can be a lot richer and more complex than that. The above deliberations serve as a useful orange road light: when we so readily make our judgements do we always know what we are talking about and are we cautiously sure we are thinking aright?

Turning now to evidence as a basis for judgement, it will properly come from our sensory perceptions, informally through personal observation, via social interaction, or formally by scientific experimentation.

There can be quite a gap between evidence for a proposition and conviction that the proposition is true. Not all cases by any means come into the category of certainty.

KNOWLEDGE

Rather a lot will be of the sort where, given the evidence, some will believe the proposition and others will withhold judgement (or even deny it, maybe).

Philosophers argue about this, and also over whether other factors can come into play legitimately; for instance, people might differ over whether to believe the evidence because of a disposition to value collecting truth above avoiding error, or the other way about. Contextual reasons may also be germane, depending on what is at stake - policy over a flood defence scheme, for instance.

Next, 'induction' is a kind of open-ended form of reasoning, where we proceed from some aspect of perceptual knowledge, via a process of extrapolation. It is much used in science.

We now list the main kinds of inductive reasoning, for there are more than one. Firstly, we generalize from the particular instance to a wider set. Secondly, there is analogy; we conclude that y has a certain property, because it is like another object, $x,$ which has that property. Finally, there is explanatory inference, where we start from a premise stating our likeliest explanation of a fact, or a state of affairs, and thus infer that the proposition expressing this explanation is true.

Even so, the idea of good inferential (inductive) reasoning is unsatisfactorily vague. The evidence may change too. And we could need to draw on many factors not mentioned in the premises. This can lead to so-termed 'inductive chains', the longer the more potential weaknesses in the links.

One related phenomenon to guard against is the so-called 'Black Swan effect'. It got its name from the fact that for many years all swans were assumed to be white, until a black one was seen in Australia, that is. So the effect is an event that is unexpected and also has a big impact on people. The tale is indeed a salutary one when it comes to the use of inductive reasoning. It graphically demonstrates that unless we know exactly what causes of a phenomenon are at work, extrapolation of past observed effects into the future may not be wise. The usual example is of the turkey still expecting to be fed each day as Christmas approaches. We need to be on our enquiry especially where phenomena are complex, with many (sometimes competing) factors at work. Prediction may be unrealistic. Risk assessment needs to decide whether to err on the side of caution.

Lastly, a battle rages between 'internalists' and 'externalists' (8.7). The former claim that any justification must come from within our minds. The kinds of thing cited are 'good reasons', found from intuitions, introspective states, memories, sense experiences, and measured against the yardstick of consistency.

Externalists deny the above and emphasize that justification comes from sources outside our mind and in the wider world.

We are faced with yet another philosophical

dichotomy. So what are the arguments and which is right? Well,both could be useful depending on context,but neither is infallible.

Regarding internalism, our beliefs need to be justified by self-awareness and 'good' reasons, and internal factors determine what those would be. The judgement comes from our mental states and the thinking going on there.

Externalism contends that the objects of thinking in the main are situated outside the thinker,and it requires a real link between knower and known so evidence of causal connections can be inferred.

(iv) Truth

We cannot leave our discussion on the nature of knowledge without reference to 'truth'. We ought to deal with the nature of truth, as well as its position within epistemology in relation to the other important concepts, like belief, knowledge, and justification.

It is generally taken for granted that truth is the main goal of epistemology, the aim of developing the beliefs which are not accidentally true only. But some would say it is knowledge we are after. Others could argue that the purpose of justification is paramount. Goals are clearly values and, according to Kvanvig, there are many epistemic ones aside from truth. Our list might include, as well as knowledge and justification, wisdom and understanding too. However, if we are looking to analyse knowledge, then truth emerges as primary.

At any rate, let us start with a condensed survey of the major theories concerning the nature of truth itself. There is an external Reality, science attests, and our truths relate to various parts of it as facts.

Possibly the most popular, and intuitively rather plausible, is the 'correspondence theory', There is said to be a 'correspondence' between true aspects of the world and propositions which relate exactly to them. Key drawbacks include correspondence being either a loose or tight concept, and that there is no necessary symmetry between language and Reality. One-to-one correspondence between features can be hard to find also.

On the 'coherence theory' of truth we find a true proposition by noting that it fits in, or 'coheres' with others. Critics will point out immediately that a whole load of untrue propositions could well cohere. Also that the truth of a proposition must surely go somewhat beyond mere coherence? In any case, the coherence theory is more like a test for truth (maybe an inessential one) than an explanation of its nature.

Coherence as a candidate for 'truth virtue', or characteristic, is unfortunately something which comes in varieties. Geometrical analogies can apply; for example, coherence could be circular, in chains, or patterned in some way. What exactly we are dealing with here is very difficult to say. There has to be mutual consistency, but relations to other epistemic properties like explanation and justification are obscure. Coherence has other problems to contend with too. There is an asymmetry whereby the fact that justification can be undermined by incoherence does not imply the reverse of coherence necessarily establishing justification. Nor can it explain the roles of experience and reason as sources of knowledge. So the author tends to regard these drawbacks as damning.

Likewise, the 'pragmatic theory' of truth falls short of providing an understanding of the concept, because all it requires is that a proposition to be true must work in practice. Such an acceptance, by the way, would have consigned the academic study of chemistry to the status of mere cookery with chemicals.

A final theory, due to Ramsey, is that truth is a 'redundant' concept; when we assert 'that p' it is just the same as saying 'p is true'.

Audi tends to push the problem of what account of the concept of truth is right into metaphysics and so away from epistemology. He is thus unconcerned with which one of the theories of truth may be correct, believing (but not demonstrating) that knowledge will be invariant under all of them.

It would seem to the present writer undue bother and dubiously sound, to have to consider two different concepts - truth and knowledge- covering similar ground,

KNOWLEDGE

and seemingly then invent some kind of complex interrelationship. The redundancy theory will thus be tentatively adopted here, along with the idea that knowledge is epistemologically prior, as well as being a complex concept to unpack.

The Architectural Structure of Knowledge

What relations exist between pieces of knowledge in our overall framework? Some have postulated the analogy of links in a chain to account for the architectural structure of knowledge. There are mathematically four types of chain - the infinite unanchored, the circular unanchored, and two anchored ones, that ending in a belief as opposed to knowledge, and that ending in the bedrock of direct knowledge.

Nothing could be known, of course, if the chain of knowledge was infinitely long. Likewise, if it was circular, some element would be causally responsible for itself - a phenomenon called the 'bootstraps problem', because you cannot haul yourself up by it. If anchored in wrong beliefs we obviously cannot get knowledge, so that only leaves the bedrock suggestion as a possibility. It then follows that any indirect knowledge we have must follow from direct knowledge of the bedrock.

Direct, grounded knowledge may come in very diverse forms, with different ways of communication, and covering numerous beliefs. Justifications may be deductive, inductive, or involve a mixture. They can be rational, or from experience. The justifications can vary a great deal in length.

But ultimately, all ends in a solid foundation to prop it up. There are dangers, which Audi thinks best averted by espousing what he calls 'moderate foundationalism'. This recognizes, quite un-dogmatically, the fallibility of both experience and reason. It should lead to a suitable humility about the limitations of what we know. Especially since it still fails to tie down precisely what knowledge is and even leaves open the question of whether there actually is any.

Assuming an affirmative answer here, since any other position would be palpably false, ridiculous even, what can we say of the modest hope for a taxonomy of subject-matter? We cannot be definitive here because the situation is changing and the race is not yet run. A trend we observe, however, is to a diversification of separate and coherent subject-areas of study and development. It is possible, nevertheless, to discern 'family resemblance groupings', depending on criteria such as methodology, or content. For example, biology has splintered off into zoology, botany, physiology and so forth, all life-related sciences. Within each such subject there is an expansion of knowledge and continued refinement to theories and methods.

Barriers to Knowledge

Obstacles in the way of our finding knowledge must

be legion, as we are aware, so the short discussion here runs the gauntlet of incomplete and unstructured listings. In their treatments of scepticism most philosophers stick to rational argument, but the barriers themselves provide formidable opposition to the possibility of knowledge too.

Starting at the frontier end, it is clear that the progress of science is slowed by such factors as problem complexity, funding shortages, and competition from more pressing or favoured research projects.

At the level of the individual, we may suffer from poor education, be cerebrally challenged, hold to divers self-deceptions, or have other interests than the acquisition of knowledge. All of us are imbued with, or at any rate unconsciously influenced by, mistaken beliefs in social traditions and mores from our family upbringing within our own society and its culture.

The distorting mirrors of ideologies will have given us additional false beliefs to contend with in fields like religion and politics.

Advertising is a very powerful modern mode of mental manipulation, of course, strengthened immeasurably by the enhanced media technologies, notably television and the internet. Some of the data we are supplied with will be correct information. Much will be deliberately false or misleadingly incomplete. So we are assailed on all sides by the commercial pressures of largely unfettered capitalism and with inadequate consumer protection to shield us from the interpretations provided by vested interests.

Scepticism

To be a sceptic in life is to be a doubter. Scepticism can apply to all manner of matters in life and any subject whatsoever. In philosophy it involves a reluctance to accept propositions, arguments, and evidence on the basis that these are not conclusive. They suspend judgement because they haven't got enough to go on. Within philosophy the concern of the present chapter, naturally, is to look at sceptical approaches to the theory of knowledge.

We all know people who tend to be sceptical. They may be late making up their minds, they may be challenging and critical with regard to authority, or to the norms and beliefs of society more widely. So it can amount to an attitudinal set. Such people may be like that with almost everything. There will be others who are only usually sceptical in relation to certain subjects or arguments.

Such variable hesitancy and distrust is mirrored in philosophy. There is a sceptical continuum over which we move, from where propositions people mostly accept as knowledge are doubted, towards a position that they are denied altogether.

Outside of this, there are confident non-sceptical philosophers who will say that knowledge does not in general require any philosophical justification.

KNOWLEDGE

The heroic approach of those epistemologists who believe in knowledge however, is to face the sceptic head on and to meet his arguments as they arise.

We shall therefore in this spirit look at strong or extreme scepticism first (8.8). It is extremely pessimistic and negative about the prospects for humans to have knowledge. Main reasons to hold the position are three-fold. Firstly, reasoning often employs chains, so one small error can take the argument astray. Worse, there may be fundamental weaknesses in our powers and/or processes of reason of which we are unaware and which, at least sometimes, will lead us into error. Secondly, we are all familiar with perceptual illusions, dreams, and other mental hallucinations. But what if these illusions, unknown to us, occur throughout our perception? Thirdly, the history of human thought sadly gives the lie to any notion that we can reliably be right. Even scientific theories are sooner or later supplanted.

Relativism is a contemporary sceptical doctrine, an example of those which claim that knowledge and objective reason are inventions of the human mind, differing from person to person. They are culture-variable and subjective.

Obviously, there is little hope of our behaving consistently in such a world, though we might not then care. Intuitively, strong scepticism will be rejected by a good many people who find it objectionable as well as impractical.

KNOWLEDGE

But, as philosophers, we need good reasons to back up our distaste. A common one is that strong scepticism is said to be self-refuted if its claims use the very concepts it says are inappropriate. 'There is no such thing as truth' is clearly false if true and true if false.

A total sceptic will, amazingly, be unconcerned about this, because refutation is another concept he will reject as non-applicable. With that, of course, also goes any pretence of the use of argument. So rational criticism is not an avenue for them. Their position is impervious to attack, but the price paid is one of extreme irrationality. So we will discount it.

Hume's argument is powerfully relevant here. Total sceptics sometimes blame socialized ways of using language for what they regard as our mistaken belief in objective truth, but he says mere linguistic conventions do not drive our behaviour. In learning to cope with Reality we come to see truth and knowledge as (fallibly) attainable through our experience and thinking.

Strong anti-sceptics, on the other hand, defend more vigorously the idea that we can obtain substantial knowledge of Reality. The environment has provided impressive tests of the evolutionary capacity of humans to adapt and survive - thus far, at any rate. Our partial harnessing of planetary conditions has shown we must be able to tap into reliable sources of knowledge. We use our intuitive sense in everyday situations and mostly get by, so we can't be going too far wrong even with that limited instrument. And our practical capacities are enormously enhanced by social cooperation and the mutual sharing of knowledge.

There is obviously much more that could be said on either side. A flavour of the debate having been given, however, it is time to move on from the extreme counsel of strong sceptical despair, whilst retaining moderate scepticism as a useful weapon in our critical armoury, hopefully to be tempered by sound judgements when we use it.

Conclusions

In conclusion, we need a framework within which to see the interrelationships between the different epistemic concepts we have been considering. The one which seems to the author to offer perhaps the best hope is due to Audi, although slightly modified. It runs something like this.

The Universe is out there, the true <u>Reality</u>, of which we can have <u>knowledge</u>. We use our senses to <u>perceive</u> it and this mediates the Reality through our minds. Because our senses are fallible, we do make mistakes, but we can and do compare notes to provide corrections. We form <u>beliefs</u> about the external world, some based on perceptions, some from other sources.

After a while our <u>memory</u> will be a store for them. Memory is also fallible, but not without reliability,

KNOWLEDGE

which differs among individuals. We also have personal knowledge gleaned by the <u>introspection</u> of our own conscious minds.

We all have <u>experience</u>, and may use our <u>reasoning</u>, but these are limited. In order to know very much about the world, we have to rely on others. So there is inevitably a socially grounded aspect to much of our knowledge.

The theoreticians have given us a flawed definition of knowledge as justified true belief, but, although it has exceptions and limitations, it is not a bad way to look at things for much of the time..

We have pointed to some of the dangers about belief - its unreliability and irrational elements, frequently grounded in childhood indoctrination and conditioning.

We have come to a view that obfuscation is the result of trying to consider truth as a complex concept and decided, on balance, that it is better to view true and false as simple dichotomies, the condition of knowledge applicable only to the former word. Truth is considered here, in summary, as a simple concept, the cardinal criterion for knowledge.

The prospects for a typography of knowledge were considered, but little insight of utility emerged beyond the merely trite.

Sources of knowledge, however, provided fertile ground for a complex discussion of the various sources,

KNOWLEDGE

none of which could be said to be impossible, or completely reliable either. The fallibility of human essays at knowledge became all too clear, despite our natural desire for matters to be otherwise. In the cases of memory and perception it was confidently hoped that scientific progress would enlighten our philosophical considerations in due course. Society was identified as another potentially fruitful area for research. We know already quite enough about testimony to make better social use of it in important arenas of public life, but why we don't is not a question which philosophy itself can appropriately address.

Looking at how knowledge holds together, and is interrelated, is, as the treatment candidly demonstrated, a matter in which analogy and metaphor abound. The 'knowledge explosion' in modern times has made the architectural structure harder to build and track, as well as rendering the prospects for any taxonomy arbitrated by purpose. The grail is still for foundations (probably within deep theory).

The deliberations on barriers to knowledge, though not philosophical as such, were provided to show how easily scepticism may be embedded, with whatever degrees of radicalism and scope.

Extreme scepticism, though not as yet convincingly refuted, was viewed as something which must be overthrown, or we might as well give up on knowledge. We could draw comfort from the realization that a thoroughgoing scepticism is almost impossible to maintain in practice, so we need take the protestations of scepticism no more seriously than sceptics themselves can do in trying to behave consistently by it.

But, whilst alive to its corrosive nature, we must not lose sight of the value of scepticism, in its milder forms, across all disciplines, as part of a healthy armoury of our critical faculties when appraising the legion claims to knowledge.

There are, of course, as we have said before, other views then these. We have encountered, for example, the tortuous and heroic efforts by philosophers to define knowledge in terms usually of belief, truth, justification, and in ways that do not fall foul of counter examples, such as we saw Gettier produce. When this happens it eventually dawns that the venture is a failure.

Williamson's way of moving on is to claim the 'primacy' of knowledge, that it has a nature not amenable to analysis and is a basic, fundamental concept in its own right (8.9). What went wrong before, according to Williamson, was partly that to try and define knowledge in terms of belief was a mistake. The state of believing could be seen as neutral between knowing and unknowing. It is better to go for evidence, then straight from that to judgement as to whether it is good enough to provide assurance of knowledge, which is a factual, world-describing state. The weakness is still the (apparently non-removable) element in justification, which is internal and mental.

KNOWLEDGE

The author goes with most of this analysis, except for the conclusion that knowledge is a primitive; we shall reserve that accolade for truth, thereby avoiding many a definitional problem for it. Nevertheless, the discussion should demonstrate the sad fact that both truth and knowledge present intractable analytical problems if viewed otherwise. It is tempting to go for a quiet life and rule out of court any truck with the idea that either truth or knowledge is a complex concept. To do so, however, seems a somewhat arbitrary convenience. It would have the effect of losing many a useful insight about knowledge that this chapter should have indicated is a rich smorgasbord.

This brings us, perhaps, to re-evaluate talk of internalism and externalism as competing for the origin of knowledge. Maybe we can do without such terms, save only to point up a spectrum, at one end of which mental processes will predominate and the other end the external world.

Lastly, a few words will be said about values and priority. Knowledge is not always regarded as a non-normative concept. It is valued and, as such, we sometimes identify the quest for it as morally virtuous. The author's stance here is to agree, but try nonetheless to leave any nobility of motivation out of it. We are looking, if you like, for some kind of objective neutrality here.

When we look at epistemology it is often taken for granted that its main purpose is to study the general nature of knowledge (seen as the principal epistemic virtue). But is it? A healthy trend in contemporary epistemology is to question this. Whilst it is obviously important, there are other epistemic virtues with strong claims to attention, like understanding, and wisdom, as well as justification, and true belief, as we have just been discussing.

Whichever aim, or aims, we are after, the assertion of some theorists is that we must begin with experience, in order to give us the basic evidence we require for the epistemic virtue we are dealing with. They contend that experience is the ultimate justification of belief, it is rational to judge by experience, which serves as guide to the truth and a way to arbitrate among disagreements. The author will end with a minor plea that we don't. That way lies woolliness and emotional clap-trap. Mediocre minds can experience as much as they like and still learn very little by it. Experience, to be usable, has to be underpinned by reflective learning and, dare we say it, that complex thing called 'knowledge'... .

9. MIND

MIND

Introduction

This chapter will attempt to address a few major problems in the philosophy of mind. First a few orientation remarks are in order.

The subject treated here is not to be confused with the philosophy of psychology, which tends to deal with methodological issues within the science of psychology (9.1).

Nor should it fall prey to what is sometimes called 'psychologism', the use of psychological arguments to try and solve philosophical problems.

In the words of Burwood, 'the dominant view in the philosophy of mind sees its task as articulating a conception of the mental consistent with the investigation of the mental by natural science' (9.2). Indeed 'we need a theory that will facilitate and promote further scientific investigation of the mind'.

In the same key, what the present chapter seeks to do is treat problems of mind in the modern context, where a revolution in the scientific understanding of mind and brain is under way, and in which several discrete subjects have to be blended. One is cognitive science, with its emphasis on the processes involved in thinking, and the artificial intelligence movement, spurred on by would-be parallels in computer development. There is also, notably, neurobiology, researching electro-chemical behaviour within the human brain.

A whole raft of mental phenomena is there to be explored. The list includes: perception, sensation, attention, emotion, intelligence, judgement, knowing_ these latter two being concepts within the purview of epistemology and discussed in an earlier chapter.

Now to quote Burwood again: 'Any modern theory in the philosophy of mind is either within the physicalist framework, or has to position itself against that framework'. So what is 'physicalism'?

'Ontologically, material entities and properties are given articulation in the terms of physical science and... this mode of articulation is privileged (i.e. is seen as fundamental). Any real distinctions in the world (at least those with empirical import) are ones captured by the theories of physical science. What is basic, therefore, is the micro world of atomic and sub-atomic physics; the macro world is ultimately the result of what obtains at the micro level. ...Physical effects have physical causes, supported by law-like generalisations that refer to physical kinds only, and whose constitutive features provide us with the requisite underlying causal mechanism.'

Physicalism also commits to the argument 'that the explanations of physical science are comprehensive.' In other words, there is no real explanation available beyond the current reaches of science, pending further scientific discovery. Philosophy should not presume to fill the gaps of

MIND

the unknown with its own empirically untestable notions.

With the foregoing preamble as guiding principle, a selection inevitably has to be made to concentrate on here. Two fundamental and prominent problems will be grappled with: the mind-body relationship, and consciousness.

The Mind-Body Problem

'Philosophy of mind, as most professionals presently working in the field conduct it, is almost exclusively concerned with the mind-body problem', says Burwood. Certainly the mind-body problem is one of the most unyielding conundrums in the whole of the philosophy of mind. Essentially, it asks how the mental processes can relate to the brain matter, given that they seem altogether different in kind.

The main theories available are dualism, philosophical behaviourism, the identity theory, eliminative materialism, and functionalism. These will each be deliberated on separately in the first instance.

We start with dualism, which originated with that father of modern philosophy, René Descartes. Unfortunately, although almost certainly and hopelessly wrong, it is so entrenched in public belief as a result of our religious history as to be virtually unshakeable.

There are varieties of dualism. 'Substance dualism',

the sort espoused by Descartes, says there are two kinds of substance - matter and mind (9.3). The former is obviously physical; the latter rather nebulous, and it may not do to dwell on the rather strange properties Descartes attributed to them.

Suffice it to say, in his day the mind was the origin of 'soul', which was believed theologically to survive the destruction of the body on death. It is this bedrock faith of the devout, with their obvious stake in the supposed existence of an after-life, that makes their belief in dualism so non-negotiable to the flock. We shall leave these aspects there, as belonging to more primitive times when the irrational held sway across society.

Returning to the argument, mind and body were nevertheless deemed able to interact causally and with the trade possibly going both ways. The differences are vaguely flagged up as to do with the mind alone being able to use language, to reason, and to be conscious.

Descartes' famous method of doubt was used. He could doubt whether he had a body, but he could not doubt that he existed. Thus, whatever he was, it was not his body. Something of a caricature of the introspection of a great thinker, perhaps, but the arguments against are very strong. Firstly, the position gives no account of how substances can interact. Secondly, it fails to explain the features of mental states.

Another version is 'property dualism', which asserts

that mental states are 'non-physical properties' of the brain, which is, of course, a physical substance having physical properties. Non-physical properties would include feelings and sensations.

Dualist theories also vary over whether they allow that the brain causes mental states, but not the opposite way round, or that mental properties can cause behaviour. Evolutionary history is against all these dualisms, since we can trace biologically how brains have developed to levels of complexity where consciousness emerges.

Another weakness is that neurobiology daily demonstrates the physical dependence on nerve cells of all mental properties. And Ockham's Razor would point to the needless complexity of dualism. But, best of all, monist materialist theories have superior explanatory force. And so most philosophers have turned their backs on dualism, as we will now do ourselves.

Yet the first materialist theory need not detain us long. For a brief spell in the twentieth century 'behaviourism' flourished, the theory that all mental states are merely tendencies to behave in certain ways in given situations. It has a superficial appeal in that there are correspondences between the mental and physical, but it is unscientific and defeatist in treating brains as 'black boxes'. That is, there are inputs in the form of stimuli from the world, and there are outputs in the guise of various behaviours, but what actually goes on in the brain is regarded like a black box, unknowns allegedly beyond our experimental powers to discover. This is defeatist. In postulating one-to-one relationships between mental state and behaviour it is being unduly simplistic, failing to provide an account of possible causal interactions between states. Nor can it deal with acting, which would lead to false predictions. Chomsky has pointed out that stimuli are not all when it comes to our responses to the world. The behaviourist view conveniently leaves out the effects of knowledge and experience. More than this, we cannot always find the stimulus. The behaviourist distaste for dealing with unobservables is unfounded, as science can successfully deal with them in other spheres, instanced by quark particles in sub-atomic physics.

A far superior candidate for solving the mind-body problem is 'reductive materialism', to be known here as 'the identity theory'. Here, mental states are just brain states.

Animals, including humans, possess a nervous system whose function is to allow them to respond appropriately to what is going on in their environments. The nerve cell, or neuron, seems to be the basic unit of the nervous system and has its own genetic instructions and biochemical equipment (9.4). It sends and receives signals, as electrical currents, via other neurons across gaps named 'synapses', aided by specialist chemicals. The number of neurons in a human brain is estimated at around one hundred billion. Each one can be connected to around 200,000 others, in ways that will differ markedly among individuals. Neurons are of various types and so are the chemical 'neurotransmitters'.

MIND

This is why the relationship of the brain to consciousness is so complex to unpack.

The relative simplicity of computers in no way matches it. Which is why Searle and others, including the author, counsel against taking the computer as a model for the brain (9.5). Both are machines, it is true, and the image is a powerful one, full of emotional and even religious overlays. But the brain is infinitely more complex, and it processes data in very different ways. Beware of this strand in Artificial Intelligence: science fiction sometimes seduces us.

In time, as we learn more and more about brain functions, we shall reveal the entire secrets of the subjective, mental world that we can. The view is economical, consistent with all we know about the animal kingdom, and being consolidated by the steady growth of knowledge supplied by the cognitive sciences. There is little danger indeed of its being overturned by a swing of fashion towards dualism. It has rivals nonetheless, and these are other theories of monist materialism, now to be explained.

There is 'functionalism', which all theorists at least take seriously, whether or not they subscribe to it. Typically, a mental state, in causing behaviour, is acting in concert with another mental state or states. It is not the same as identity theory because here there is no fixed correspondence between given physical and mental states. Nor is it like behaviourism; it does not try to match and fix a relation between an environmental input and an output of behaviour.

MIND

The deep difficulty is to conceive of how the very distinctive psychological states in the mind can emanate from a physical base such as the brain. Burwood explains where the theory of functionalism can help, 'probably the most popular theory in the philosophy of mind today'. 'What functionalism does is insert an intermediate level of description, the functional level, between the psychological and the physical'. There are different versions of functionalism, but 'the one that is in most accord with the overall physicalist project....is reductive functionalism. On this account psychological states reduce to non-mental functional definitions discoverable by scientific psychology. These, in turn, 'supervene' on a given physical base. So, the essence of any given psychological state is that it is an inner causal state of an organism with a particular functional role. However, Burwood does sound a cautionary note: 'functionalism too has problems encompassing all the mind features in one over-arching theory'.

It has in addition to convince us that 'supervenience' explicates more than it obfuscates. 'Supervenience' is a disputed concept, especially (though not exclusively) used in the philosophy of mind to explain how the mental and the physical relate. Specifically, a mental event is not identical with the physical state of the brain, but will 'supervene on' the physical properties concerned. Two people could have exactly the same mental state, but be in different physical states, nonetheless.

Searle explains further: 'to say that a phenomenon

MIND

A is supervening on a phenomenon B is to say that it is totally dependent on B in such a way that any change in the A property has to be correlated with a change in the B property. It is commonly said that consciousness is supervening on brain processes. The basic idea is that there can be no changes in mental states without corresponding changing in brain states.' Such is called 'non-reductive materialism'. 'The idea of supervenience is to give a completely materialistic account without in any sense trying to eliminate consciousness.' Searle accepts supervenience, and that it is causal, but challenges the concept for its failure to add any explanation of brain states causing mental states.

The arguments against functionalism are not necessarily compelling, and it is likely that its sophistication will increase as a result of ongoing research programmes. Even so, its ambitions will not produce a complete theory of the mind, as it concentrates on the communication and information side, not the biology of the brain.

Next is 'eliminative materialism', kept until last owing to its extreme nature. Bluntly, it is the doctrine which says mental states do not exist. And it is so radical the justification for it had better be good. A leading proponent is Churchland, who disparages ordinary talk of mental states as mere 'folk psychology', which gets nowhere and which is destined to be replaced in time by the scientific findings of neuropsychology (9.6). Commonsense and private introspection, he predicts, will give way to informed and insightful language which will do what folk psychology cannot, explain key phenomena - emotions, desires, beliefs, sensations, and perceptions, memory, sleep, intelligence. Obviously some practitioners have fought back, defending folk psychology as a basis for working understandings and with the potential to be useful, allied to scientific research. The issue remains unresolved, though more will have to be said in our conclusions.

At this time we turn in lieu of answers to another, related, and seemingly intractable imponderable-consciousness.

Consciousness

The problem of consciousness could be thought of as a sub-division of the more general mind-body problem. It has defeated all comers so far in satisfactorily trying to explain how it comes about.

'Consciousness' is a term that could be used of elementary as well as advanced animals, so long as they can feel pain, for example. The stronger sense, to be studied here, is better called 'self-consciousness', and might be confined only to humans, or at least some of the larger mammals, particularly if it requires a level of rational capability. Self-consciousness is where a being becomes conscious of itself, of course.

Smart argues that conscious experiences are just brain processes (9.7). Not many other philosophers would agree with him. Our ordinary language use might suggest otherwise, yet language can mislead and here it is not giving a scientific account. Again, experiences are not reported as though they were something spatial, unlike brain processes, although this could just reflect ignorance within historical usage. If conscious experiences are emergent properties of brain processes, the problem reasserts itself as how to account for the emergence. Smart dismisses it as simply our description of a sensation like my pain. In a sense what we mean and what we say are irrelevant.

Sellars may perhaps be understood as holding that in a system of sufficient structural complexity (like, say, the human brain) new fundamental principles come into being, or 'emerge'. These have a physical origin yet will probably require a whole new language of tightly defined concepts by which to take forward and develop insights and understanding. Quite possibly, all talk of 'consciousness' as we understand it will be jettisoned in the process.

We saw earlier that supervenience is controversial, but it has similarity with a very important scientific phenomenon just now referred to - emergence. According to Holland, a leading exponent, emergence is a very useful guiding principle with much unexplored potential (9.8). Essentially, emergence occurs in systems that attain a certain level of complexity, at which point properties 'emerge' which cannot be revealed by inspection of the laws governing their components. The question is: can the emergence of consciousness in the brain once it reaches sufficient complexity explain its connection with firing neurons and their interactions? Holland highlights the gravity of the problem '…we have neither theories, models, nor artifacts wherein each neuron simultaneously interacts with thousands of others via synapses (and networks), and wherein the connections among agents involve so many feedback loops that a single agent may belong to hundreds or thousands of loops… .' What we now know of machines provides little guidance to machines of that complexity. Extrapolation in such circumstances is, at best, mere speculation.

Searle agrees with Crick that consciousness needs the scientific study formerly shunned and that a likely approach would be to try to correlate it with neural states. If you can induce a particular neural state, and show that it is always correlated with a certain conscious experience, then you have evidence of a real causal link between the neural state and the conscious experience. In the same way, other neural states and their correlations to consciousness could be tested until a map could be built up. A theory might then be devised to refine a developing model. We do not know, however, whether it can be done. We don't even know whether neurons constitute the basic functional unit. Are there more fundamental sub-neuronic entities? Does neuron architecture - the network structure - hold the key?

Another approach is to compare consciousness with the unconscious, where we find psychological brain processes with no conscious manifestation. What we would be trying to do there is narrow down those processes where information is only a feature of consciousness.

MIND

Weiskrantz showed that people under psychological test, who did not have any conscious vision, could point to objects and guess their shape and movement far more than could be explained by mere chance (9.9). This 'blind sight' has now been extended to 'blind smell' and 'blind touch'. It seems that although the brain region normally responsible for particular conscious processes has been damaged, some kind of electrochemical re-routing can occur with partial compensation for the disability. That would suggest prospects for finding a mechanism overseeing interactions in different regions of the brain.

Two particular developments in understanding the biology of the brain are significant here. Firstly, discoveries that there are spontaneous electrical rhythms which can be recorded and measured, in sleep and conscious states, led to defining three states of 'consciousness' - waking, dream sleep, and slow-wave (deep) sleep. Secondly, discrete regions of the brain were found to be the sources of control of certain bodily functions. For instance, regulation of breathing and the heart are associated with the lower part of the brain stem, whereas the contents of consciousness are the responsibility of the cerebral hemispheres.

To complicate matters, Damasio points out that as the brain is attached to a body, as such it is subject to hormonal and other chemical interactions which alter states of consciousness (9.10). Looking at evolution, we see animals of very variable brain capacities, of course. At the more primitive end they seem to have a dim awareness of the present and a very short memory. The higher mammals display much 'extended consciousness' beyond the primitive 'core', evidence of a dynamic, evolving interaction between the creature and its environment, the physical, and also the social. These are learning, evaluative features, supplied by an improving memory of accumulated experiences, into an organised, future-looking, self-centred, but socially- adjusted mindset.

Thomas Nagel, in his famous essay 'What is it like to be a bat?', graphically illustrated a widespread philosophical worry, namely that whatever state of completion we reach in our understanding of the brain, it will still tell us nothing about our subjective experience, that leap into consciousness and awareness of the private mind (9.11). Ultimately, the attitude is a counsel of despair for scientific research and one that could harbour dualism.

Opposed are philosophers like Dennett and Churchland, who are physicalists of one kind or another. Eliminativists (Churchland, we saw, is one) regard the concept of consciousness as confused and dispensable. Reductionists concede consciousness is useful, but entirely physical in nature, all equating to neural processes.

Intentionality

There is probably a need to say a little finally about the concept of intentionality, considered by some to pose a third major problem in the philosophy of mind. Note that intentionality is nothing much to do with the word 'intentional' when the latter is used to mean that some action was done deliberately. A lot of confusion revolves around whether we have two ideas or one when we refer to 'intentionality' and 'intensionality'. No distinction will be made in our consideration here and we shall follow Searle in spelling the word with a 't'.

Look at the statements 'the belief that…' or 'the hope that.' They are 'propositional attitudes', because they refer to specific propositions and strike particular attitudes towards them. These mental stances show 'intentionality', which means to say they point beyond themselves to something external, features of the world in fact.

Searle contends: 'the problem of intentionality is second only to the problem of consciousness as a supposedly difficult, or perhaps impossibly difficult, problem in the philosophy of mind.' He distinguishes three questions: 'first, how is intentionality possible; … second,…, how is content (of intentional states) determined; and thirdly, how does the whole system of intentionality work?'

By the way, we can use the word 'information' in place of intentionality, provided we remember that it is often ambiguous as between the external object observed and that gleaned by the mental sense of observing.

No further treatment will be given here, except to observe that Searle started out as a philosopher in the Oxford language movement, a disciple of Austin, author of the classic 'How to do Things with Words.' It is at least plausible that the problem belongs better in the field of semantics than within the present (essentially ontological) discussion.

Conclusions

It is now time to put together brief concluding remarks on this most vexatious of topics. Mind has a key collection of philosophical problems owing to its being at the nexus where the inner, subjective human experiences meet the outer world of objective reality. It is therefore not surprising that it holds perennial fascination. Palpably, we are all concerned by the findings. And here, unless hopelessly bigoted, we are bound to be let down by the paucity of current knowledge.

We will start by a reiteration of our conviction that philosophy of mind must be compatible with the results of physical science. If not, it is likely to be bunkum. The present author also believes that philosophy will have little to contribute to our expanding knowledge of mind in the future, having done such a thoroughly bad job of it thus far and generated additional confusions in the process.

Looking anew then at the problems discussed in the chapter, and taking the last of them first, what are we to say of intentionality, that mysterious 'aboutness' that philosophers (not by any means all) postulate of the connection between our thoughts and objects in the world?

MIND

It would seem to be a strong candidate to be one of the invented confusions we spoke about.

Intentionality might not be a respectable philosophical concept. After all, it is said to be a relation between a conscious event and something out in the world. But we can easily think about entities that do not exist. So it cannot be a relation and may even be a nonsense.

The big trouble with intentionality is that it does nothing to uncover or systematize the manners in which the outside world and the mind interact. These are in large number and include, according to Scruton, perceptions, beliefs, desires, emotions, thoughts, and imagination. Just what out there is constructed by our human faculties and requirements is profoundly moot still and is going to produce clouds of fog.

Moving back to the start to recall the mind-body problem, we have already seen the shortcomings of dualism. Once we decide on a monist position, however, we are confronted with various plausible choices, probably the least convincing and explanatory of which is behaviourism.

The functionalist position seemed promising, yet introduced the dubious and complicating concept of supervenience, in need of further evidence on its own account.

What we are left with, substantially, are eliminative materialism and the identity theory. But the former seems to depend on the abolition of all so-called 'folk psychology'; in other words, the kind of sloppy ideas and loose concepts ordinary people use when talking about the mind in everyday conversation. That idea in principle can be tested, of course. Rigorous research might inform us in time as to whether the popular terms can be used scientifically, if sharpened up in application, or whether the mind is so alien that we are being hopelessly misled. It may not be entirely guesswork to doubt that all of them will be found so wanting. After all, whilst folk psychology could be falsely born, of dodgy intuitions and traditional superstitions, it might also conceivably reflect voices of experience and wisdom. At any rate, it continues to be helpful to ordinary mortals.

So the temptation is to plump for the identity theory and, perhaps in so doing, narrow our truth-seeking ambitions, reflected in the light of realism. For, even though science may one day have developed a very complete understanding of brain function, there will probably still be an unexplained gap where mental properties emerge from the physical. Philosophers despair. Yet this is a respectable eventuality. If it is a brute fact of nature it cannot be unravelled. Ruing it would be fatuous.

Third and last, we need to come to terms with the problem of consciousness. When we remember that there is much going on in our unconscious brains, and compare differences of apparent mental ability between the animals, we possibly conclude that consciousness is part of a continuum, a gradation of electrochemical activity in nature.

MIND

What we can also say, along with Honderich, is that consciousness is a real biological phenomenon (unlike probably intentionality or supervenience which are unproven concepts), and that it has an element of subjectivity to it (9.12). When you think about yourself, you can become aware of your inner attitudes, moods, emotions, beliefs, wishes, and sundry other internal states of mind besides.

You might remonstrate with disappointment that none of these deliberations has brought us very far. And you would be right. Some philosophers have thus been prompted to claim we should start all over again from scratch, that the problem of consciousness requires a fresh and novel approach with new parameters. Just what that investigation could amount to sadly remains to be seen. But if it is not led by scientists it will get nowhere is the penultimate contention.

The answers to consciousness could well be the answer to emergence, if it is possible to have a general one for a phenomenon that is so widespread. The matter might simply boil down to false perception. As consciousness is such a big deal, such a bedrock part of what it is to be human, we insist on pursuing its 'mystery'. But where emergence is not personal, where it concerns a non-human issue like how properties of a chemical compound emerge vastly different from those of its constituent elements, we pay little attention to finding a solution. We concentrate on the contrary on what is more realistic to ascertain; in this case a full characterization of the elements and the compound separately. In the process we have had to develop new concepts for dealing, for instance, with the mechanisms by which compounds react, operating with technical terms we did not have before. Which is one reason why the fact of emergence sometimes seems so abrupt and discontinuous. We can fall foul of the wrong metaphors, including those of barriers and hierarchy.

PHILOSOPHICAL ESSAYS

NOTES

2. WISDOM

2.1 Thesaurus of the English Language, Harper Collins Publishers, Glasgow, Third Edition, 2008.

2.2 Tapper, Josh, 'Wisdom does come with age', The Guardian Weekly, 27th August, 2010.

2.3 Ryan, Sharon, The Stanford Encyclopaedia of Philosophy, 2007.

2.4 de Botton, Alain, The Consolations of Philosophy, Hamish Hamilton, London, 2000.

2.5 Armstrong, John, Conditions of Love, Allen Lane, The Penguin Press, London, 2002.

2.6 Comte-Sponville, André, The Great Virtues, Vintage, Random House, London, 2002.

2.7 Butler, Gillian, and Hope, Tony, Manage Your Mind, Oxford University Press,1995.

2.8 Cunningham, Dean, Pure Wisdom, Prentice Hall Life, Pearson Education Limited, Harlow, 2011.

2.9   Maxwell, Nicholas, 'Knowledge or wisdom?', The
      Philosophy Magazine, Third Quarter, 2013.

3.   APPROACHES

3.1   Buckingham, Will; Burnham, Douglas; Hill, Clive;
      King, Peter J; Marenbon, John; Week , Marcus,
      The Philosophy Book, Dorling-Kindersley, London,
      2011.

3.2   Wilson, Edward O., Consilience - The Unity of
      Knowledge, Abacus, 1999.

3.3   White, Alan, Toward a Philosophical Theory of
      Everything, Bloomsbury Academic, London, 2014.

3.4   Verene, Donald Phillip, Speculative Philosophy,
      Lexington Books, USA, 2008.

4.   CORE

4.1   Ayer, A.J., Language, Truth and Logic, Penguin
      Books, Middlesex, 1971.

4.2   Effingham, Nikk, An Introduction to Ontology,
      Polity Press, 2013.

4.3   Lowe, E.J., A Survey of Metaphysics, Oxford
      University Press, 2002.

5.   THINKING

5.1   Schwartz, Stephen P., A Brief History of Analytic
      Philosophy, John Wiley and Sons, Inc., 2012.

5.2   Alexander, Joshua, Experimental Philosophy, Polity
      Press, Cambridge, 2012.

5.3 Williamson, T, 'Philosophical Intuitions and
      Scepticism about judgement', Dialectica 58,109-
      155, 2004.

5.4   Baggini, Julian, and Fosl, S., Peter, The
      Philosopher's Tool Kit, Blackwell Publishing Ltd.,
      Oxford, 2003.

5.5   Nozick, Robert, Philosophical Explanation, Harvard
      University Press, Cambridge, Massachusetts, 1981.

5.6   Michalos, Alex, C., Improving your Reasoning,
      Prentice Hall, 1970.

5.7   Flew, Anthony, Thinking About Thinking, Fontana/
      Collins, 1975.

5.8   Warburton, Nigel, Thinking from A to Z, Routledge,
      Third Edition, 2007.

5.9   Watts, Duncan J., Everything is Obvious, Atlantic
      Books, London, 2011.

5.10 Whyte, James, Bad Thoughts - A Guide to Clear
      Thinking, Corvo Books, 2003.

5.11 Sutherland, Stuart, Irrationality, Penguin Books,
      London, 1994.

5.12 Greenspan, Neil, 'The Ever-Expanding Kingdom of
      Bull', Philosophy Now, May/June, 2011.

5.13 Dennett, Daniel, 'Handy tools for easier thinking',
      New Scientist, 19th September, 2013.

5.14 Scruton, Roger, Modern Philosophy, Pimlico,
      Random House, London, 2004.

5.15 Alexander, Joshua, Experimental Philosophy, Polity
      Press, Cambridge, 2012.

6. THINGS

6.0 Effingham, Nikk, An Introduction to Ontology,
     Polity Press, Cambridge, 2013.

6.1 Armstrong, D.M, Sketch for a Systematic
     Metaphysics, Oxford University Press, 2010.

6.2 Strawson, Peter, F., Analysis and Metaphysics,
     Oxford University Press, 1992.

6.3 Lowe, E.J., A Survey of Metaphysics, Oxford
     University Press, 2002.

6.4 Scruton, Roger, Modern Philosophy, Pimlico,
     Random House, London, 2004.

6.5 Goodman, Nelson, Ways of Worldmaking, Hackett
     Publishing Co., 1978.

6.6 Armstrong, David, A World of States of Affairs,
     Cambridge University Press, First Edition, 1997.

6.7 Sider, Theodore, and Conee, Earl, Riddles of
     Existence, Oxford University Press, First Edition,
     2005.

6.8 Lowe, E.J., A Metaphysical Foundation for Natural
     Science, Oxford, Clarendon Press, 2006.

7. LOGIC

7.1 Proudfoot, Michael, and Lacey, A.R., The Dictionary
     of Philosophy, Routledge, Abingdon, Fourth Edition,
     2010.

7.2 McGinn, Colin, Logical Properties, Oxford
     University Press, 2000.

7.3 Lowe, E.J., 'Philosophical Logic', Durham
     University.

7.4 Scruton, Roger, Modern Philosophy, Pimlico, 1994.

7.5 Ferguson, Stephen, 'What is the Philosophy of Mathematics', Philosophy Now, 1997.

7.6 Sardar, Ziauddin, and Ravetz, Jerry, Mathematics: A Graphic Guide, Totem Books, 2001.

7.7 Körner, Stephan, The Philosophy of Mathematics, Courier Dover Publications, 1986.

7.8 Barrow, John D., New Theories of Everything, Oxford University Press, 2007.

7.9 Davis, Philip J., The Mathematical Experience, Birkhäuser, Boston USA, 1995.

8. KNOWLEDGE

8.1 The Routledge Dictionary of Philosophy, Routledge, Abingdon, Oxon, Fourth edition, 2010.

8.2 Audi, Robert, Epistemology, Routledge, Abingdon, Oxon, Third edition, 2011.

8.3 Goldman, Alvin I., Pathways to Knowledge - Private and Public, Oxford University Press, 2002.

8.4 Teichman, Jenny, and Evans, Katherine C., Philosophy: A Beginner's Guide, Blackwell

Publishing, Oxford, Third edition, 1999.

8.5   Pritchard, Duncan, What is this Thing called Knowledge?, Routledge, Abingdon, Oxon, Second edition, 2010.

8.6   Greenspan, Neil, 'Judgements of Similarity', The Philosophy Magazine, Third Quarter, 2013.

8.7   Steup, Matthias, Turri, John, Sosa, Ernest, editors, Contemporary Debates In Epistemology, Wiley Blackwell, Chichester, West Sussex, 2014.

8.8   Morton Adam, A Guide Through the Theory of Knowledge, Blackwell, Oxford, Second edition, 1997.

8.9   Williamson, Timothy, Knowledge and its Limits, Oxford University Press, 2000.

9.   MIND

9.1   Proudfoot, Michael, and Lacey, A.R., The Routledge Dictionary of Philosophy, Fourth Edition, Routledge, Abingdon, 2010.

9.2   Burwood, Stephen, 'Philosophy of Mind', in Shand, John, Editor, Fundamentals of Philosophy, Routledge, London, 2003.

9.3   Ravenscroft, Ian, Philosophy of Mind, Oxford
      University Press, 2005.

9.4   Zeman, Adam, 'The Problem of Consciousness',
      Prospect Magazine, December, 1999.

9.5   Searle, John R., Mind - A Brief Introduction, Oxford
      University Press, 2004.

9.6   Churchland, Paul, Matter and Consciousness,
      Princeton, New Jersey, 1983.

9.7   Scruton, Roger, Modern Philosophy, Pimlico,
      Random House, London, 2004.

9.8   Holland, John H, Emergence: From Chaos to Order,
      Oxford University Press, 1998.

9.9   Weiskrantz, L, Blindsight, Oxford University Press,
      1986.

9.10 Damasio, Antonio, The Feeling of What Happens:
      Body, Emotion and the Making of Consciousness,
      Heinemann, 2000.

9.11 Nagel, Thomas, Mortal Questions, Cambridge
      University Press, New Edition, 1991.

9.12 Honderich, Ted and Papineau, David, 'Introducing
      Consciousness', Philosophy Now, October/
      November, 2000.